DANCE of the BROKEN HEART

DANCE of the

BROKEN HEART

A Family Love Story

John & Patti Thompson

ABINGDON PRESS
Nashville

DANCE OF THE BROKEN HEART

Library of Congress Cataloging-in-Publication Data

Thompson, John, 1950–
    Dance of the broken heart.

    1. Remarriage—Religious aspects—Christianity. 2. Thompson, John, 1950–   . 3. Thompson, Patti. I. Thompson, Patti. II. Title.
BV838.T47 1986   248.8'4   86-20599
    ISBN 0-687-10080-1 (alk. paper)

MANUFACTURED BY THE PARTHENON PRESS AT
NASHVILLE, TENNESSEE, UNITED STATES OF AMERICA

We dedicate this book to our children.

It may yet be several years before they realize the full implications of what we have written—but some day they will. And then they will know that throughout these blessed and difficult years of blending we have loved them with all of our hearts and have tried to make choices that would bring healing to each of them.

Acknowledgments

We thank Mary Ruth Howes for her steady head and quiet wisdom. She edited us with humor as well as intelligence.

We also thank our dear pals Peter and Barbara Jenkins for helping us birth the whole thing. In deference to Peter's strange mix of Southern "good-ole-boy" ease and New York literary agent big talk, we simply say thanks "Swifty Bob" for a job well done.

Cindy Thompson moved into our home for five weeks to type the manuscript, to talk, to pray over ideas, and to encourage us. Dear Cindy, there would have been no book without you, as it would have lingered in the air somewhere between dreams and reality. Thank you so much.

Thank you to Jayne Ann Woods and Trish Hamilton, who prayed . . . and prayed . . . and prayed. What wonderful friends they are to us!

And to Caroline and Alice (our mothers), we give loving thanks for your willingness to leave your own little nests and come ride herd over ours while we wrote.

Finally, to the wonderful people of St. Bartholomew's Episcopal Church, who have been and are family to us, we thank you all for your mighty prayers and love.

Bless you all,

John and Patti Thompson

Contents

Foreword

*Y*ou may kiss the bride," the United Methodist minister said through a broad smile. John Thompson leaned forward, a little nervous, and gently kissed his beautiful and famous bride, Patti, ex-daughter-in-law of Oral Roberts. She opened her arms and held her groom close enough so he could see the million stars in her eyes. Their lips met. For them, it was a new day, a fresh start for two hurting adults, both weary and wounded from past marriages.

We were honored to be there on their wedding day and to lend our support to John and Patti, who needed blessing, not criticism, and everyone's helping hand, not more hurt. They looked radiant and wonderfully whole. The nagging hope of everyone who stood watching was that John and Patti would have the "perfect" marriage . . . this time.

From the outside, everything looked great. But behind closed doors, John and Patti began crumbling before they got off to a good start! The pressures of two of his children and two of hers, their separate but talented roller-coaster musical careers, untold secrets from the past, and being thrown into the public eye were too much!

This is a story of grit and love, of courage and fear, and of a bull-dog determination to hang on, not to let go of God or of each other. We see John and Patti fight the good fight for themselves and for their grafted-together family. Through their struggles, we begin to see seldom-discussed insights about the covenant relationship of marriage and holy truths that have been ignored and forgotten.

John and Patti bravely show us themselves, both good and bad, and tell us of a way through the darkness. Their problems are echoed in the homes of millions of other divorced and remarried couples, all of whom are crying and fighting, adjusting and hurting and trying to blend everyone into a family unit again. They all want wholeness and stability and harmony, but how, how, how?

This is not another in a long line of "how-to" books written by someone who's never "been there." John and Patti know that with God's help there are workable solutions. Their book offers help and healing for broken lives. Theirs is a love story that takes you by the hand and says, "Beloved, let us dance again."

PETER AND BARBARA JENKINS
SWEET SPRINGS FARM
SPRING HILL, TENNESSEE

Introduction

With the advent of the nuclear age, our perception of destruction has grown beyond our previous imaginations. The writers and artists of this era, from George Orwell to George Lucas, have given us scenes of despair and annihilation, enabling us to visualize the end of humankind. On our movie and television screens, we have seen entire planets disappear from existence. We have sped with Luke Skywalker across the gray, smoking terrain of a distant planet on which only a handful of inhabitants could be found alive. And we have witnessed first-hand what the world might look like "the day after." Yet daily an event occurs that far outweighs the splitting of the atom, in terms of potential destructive power: the breaking of a human heart.

The heart—the most vulnerable of God's creations, yet the strongest. It is at the heart that God chooses to link himself with us, and it is at the heart that Satan aims every force that he can marshal, knowing that every linking spells his own defeat.

Satan must have trembled that day in Nazareth when one of the local young men stood up and read the ancient words of Isaiah:

"The Spirit of the Lord God is upon me. He chose me to tell the Good News to poor people. He sent me to preach freedom to captives and to help blind people see again. He sent me to lift up broken-hearted people and to announce the welcome year of the Lord God." Jesus rolled up the scroll and gave it back to the keeper. Then Jesus sat down. Every person in the synagogue was watching Jesus very closely. Jesus began to speak to them. He said, "While you heard me reading these words just now, the words were coming true!" (Luke 4:18-21 SEB)

Jesus had just announced God's program—to heal and mend the broken hearts of God's creation.

This is not a how-to book, nor is it a how-not-to book. It is simply a love story about a family in which the grace of God has begun the collective binding of some very broken hearts. However, this is not "the latest" or "most definitive" statement about brokenness. It is only one of many. We offer no easy solutions, because we have found none. But we have seen God keep His word, sometimes painfully, and we have experienced His forgiveness and restoration. We realize it is pretty bold to write of our journey into wholeness while only having been on this road together for three and a half years. But the grace God has offered us would apply to the problems of a marriage of three days or of thirty years, for hurt in relationships doesn't necessarily cease even after the celebration of the silver anniversary. Though our hearts are still on the mend, we have no fear of stepping out in joy—not limping or with crutches, but dancing. Dancing because we have seen, with those in Nazareth's synagogue, the scripture fulfilled in our hearing.

To him who is able to make the broken heart dance,

Praise!

DANCE of the BROKEN HEART

PART I

"Then shall the lame man leap like a hart"
Isaiah 35:6

It was just like in the movies . . .
  The music of yet-to-be-spent euphoria underscores
  the picture of him reaching,
              longing,
                  running toward her,
  hoping that somewhere out there she did indeed exist.

She, too, reaches and longs . . .
and at the hint that there is no "him"
                she weeps.

They run harder and harder
through deserts and valleys,
over hills and mountains,
                through war zones . . .
                minefields . . .
                whitened fields . . .
                their chosen fields . . .
hoping that their paths will intersect,
that at last they'll find in the other
a place for "home" . . .
for both had lost it along the way.

  Finally in the third decade of the journey
  she sees a figure on the horizon.
  Could it be?
  He comes closer.
  Could it be?

  Only after their joyously long embrace
  do they pull back
  each to gaze at the beloved.

  She said, ". . . Oh, my love, the scars
  of the journey have marred
  your beauty."
  As he dropped his head,
  he noticed that there were stones
  embedded in her feet.
  He spoke, ". . . and my dearest,
  you are limping. Here,
  let me carry you.
  We have yet a long way to go."

                                        P.T.

1

The Meeting

Patti

I took a last brief tour of the house just to make sure everything was party-ready. The house smelled of flowers, fragrant candles, and my perfume. I do love a party, and the annual Gospel Music Dove Awards ceremony was as good a reason as any to throw a celebration. My friends would all be descending upon this old house following tonight's events. The party had become something of a habit we had developed through the several years we had been attending the Doves. The old lady that Christi, Juli, and I lived in pulled herself up grandly and proudly displayed her one hundred forty years of existence. She was never more beautiful than at party time; no doubt these foot-thick walls and twelve-foot ceilings had graciously received hundreds of people for a great number of gala events through the years since the Civil War.

During the Civil War, this house watched as the Battle of Franklin was bloodily fought almost on her front stoop. According to local legend, the dug-out cellar was used as a makeshift field hospital. The Courtney-Bradford House, as she is called, must have seen some intense fighting, indeed, because as she was being renovated some fifteen years ago, cannonball fragments were found still lodged in the thick brick wall that separated the entry foyer from a porch, which has lately become a sunroom.

Back in my dressing room, I glanced at my hair and makeup, poofing up the silk organza ruffles that surrounded my shoulders and throat. Yes, I looked all done up, indeed. The stunning black gown made me feel truly royal, especially since it was a gift from Contessa Maragen Chinigo, a friend from Tulsa days. I had always cherished that gown. Not only was it fabulous, but also the dear lady who had given it to me.

I grabbed my white mink coat and floated down the long spiral staircase to the front hall just as the doorbell signaled the arrival of my escort. *Will I never get used to that loud ringing?* I thought. The antique wind-up bell that sits like a belly button in the center of the front door announces visitors so loudly that even after years of hearing it, I still jump.

I opened the door with hopes that perhaps my friend's mood had changed and that tonight we could resolve our differences and carry on with what might be a promising friendship. I needn't have wasted my hopes. His polite, but rather cold, greeting reaffirmed my belief that this date would be our last.

Well, even if this was our "swan song" date, we did make a smashing couple. As always, he was elegantly turned out. It was such a terrible shame that we were so entirely ideologically mismatched, because in most other ways he perfectly fit my stringent list of forty-three criteria that must be met by the man who would be my future mate. During these past single years, I kept hoping to find someone who would be a suitable mate physically, intellectually, and spiritually, one who would nurture and soothe my battle-worn children, and especially one who would insulate us from everything and everyone who had ever hurt us. That perfect man existed somewhere . . . didn't he? For a while, I thought the man who was my date tonight could have been the perfect man. Alas, it was not to be. As the curtain went up on the ceremony at Nashville's Tennessee Performing Arts Center, another was going down on this brief, sadly doomed relationship.

I absorbed myself in the excitement of the night's events. Several of my friends were nominated for awards; Russ and Tori Taff, long-time friends of mine, seemed to be nominated for just about everything. I am not altogether sure that a Grammy Awards-type of event is appropriate for those involved in gospel music. Perhaps, in reality, the awards are a contradiction in terms. But even if that is so, I eagerly waited to hear the names of the winners, hoping Russ and Tori would be among them. Seeing those you love rewarded for their excellence is a warming experience—even though this ceremony never passes that I don't feel some tinge of sorrow. Quite apart from what questions I may have regarding the legitimacy of these film-colony-style awards, nevertheless I ached at not belonging to the circle of receivers. Belonging was still an urgent need.

One by one the winners walked to the stage to collect their bronze statues formed in the likeness of a dove. For every one winner there were, perhaps, thousands of unnamed singers, writers, and ministers who stood invisibly beside the awardees, co-laborers in a very ripe field.

I applauded loudly as Russ won the male vocalist of the year award for 1983. His singing had often given voice to some unsung feeling deep within my own soul.

Mayor Richard Fulton of Nashville was being introduced. *What a good stroke,* I thought, *to have the mayor of Music City give out the most prestigious award, the one for Song of the Year.* ". . . and this year's Song of the Year is . . ." The crowd stilled as he tore open the white envelope . . . "El Shaddai. Composer John Thompson and lyricist Michael Card. Whole Armor Publishing. Publishers John Thompson and Randy Scruggs."

The room swelled with applause as the threesome walked toward the mayor to receive their dove statuettes for their song, made so famous by gospel's own Amy Grant.

John

I am a composer. Sometimes my songs are signposts to me; I can look back on them as definite transition points in my life. They often contain the markings of some deep struggle of the soul that surfaces as a melody long before my mind can express it in actual thoughts or words.

One night, I awakened from a restless sleep with a very real desire to know more about God and with a simple melody running through my mind. This was a dry time in my life, much like the deserts that some of the Old Testament characters lived through. I went downstairs to the piano and played the melody I was hearing, and for several hours I worked on the composition. It was as though God became very close to me, and I was comforted. I now look back and see that God, hearing the inner cries of my heart, was beginning to reveal himself to me as the covenant God.

I could not think of any lyrics appropriate for the melody, so I stored it with many others in my memory, knowing that I would get back to it later. I played the melody for several people—lyricists, potential co-writers—but nothing clicked. Then I played it for my friend Michael Card. I didn't know what the right lyrics should be, I told him. I just knew that the song was about God Almighty. Michael told me that the Hebrew name for God Almighty is *El Shaddai*. By the next morning, he had finished the entire lyric.

Now, two years later, I found myself as one of five nominees for the song of the year award, sitting in a packed auditorium waiting for the winner to be announced. The five nominated songs were performed during the course of the program, and as Amy Grant began to sing "El Shaddai," I mentally ran through the two years that had elasped since I wrote the melody to which I was now listening. For one thing, I had seen the break-up of my second marriage, and I had been placed in the category of weekend father. I hate that phrase. It is *not* what I am. I love my children, Matthew and Jessica, all the time, seven days a week. I am their father; their love never questioned that. I had asked God to forgive me. I had very little interest in the statuettes that were being presented. My mind was desperate for peace. That is what I would have liked for someone on that stage to have handed me—peace.

Patti

So that's John Thomspon . . . well. My thoughts drowned out the acceptance speeches. I was remembering a phone conversation about seven or eight months prior to this festive April evening—with John Thompson. At Michael Card's urging, John had called me, out of interest, curiosity, or just to placate his nagging friend, I wasn't sure. And in spite of the relatively small size not only of Nashville but also of the gospel music industry, I had never before had a chance to meet or even see John Thompson. It was with much interest, then, that I now matched a face with the voice I had heard on the other end of the phone line.

I remembered our conversation with delight. How completely disarming his phone presentation had been! He'd sounded funny, intelligent, warm, sensitive, straightforward—utterly delightful. He had told me that he was a writer and producer, but I couldn't recall his particularly sounding like the music-business type. He said that he had just bought a house in Belle Meade. Well, that had been a good sign. Belle Meade is a fashionable, rather stable, part of Nashville. People who live there are stereotyped as being wealthy, well-bred, and largely Republican. To my ears it had a kind of homey ring.

John had also sounded unusually sensitive toward God. It wasn't often that I had conversations that were at once humorous, spiritual, intelligent, carefree, and intense. The only thing ordinary about it was that we had concluded our long chat with the obligatory music-biz closer, "Let's have lunch." And that was that. In spite of the fact that I was probably as cute and charming as I had ever been on the phone, I never again heard from John Thompson. I guess we both had had other fish to fry.

As John carried his Dove statuette back to his seat, I looked at him carefully. With the tuxedo and the six-foot or so frame, he was not too unlike most of the men in the hall. But his face was wonderful. Keenly expressive blue eyes captured my attention. There wasn't the slightest bit of affectation about him. He seemed to be a perfectly centered person in a somewhat skewed world, giving off an aura of unrehearsed calm. His visual persona matched the kindness that I remembered in his phone call. As for the events of the evening, he seemed to be taking it all in with a grain of salt. I found that interesting enough to fuel the desire for a closer look at this guy who never phoned back. Apparently, he had taken me with a grain of salt as well.

My date had people to see, so as soon as we got to the lobby following the awards ceremony, he excused himself and began to work the room. I stood unattended in a sea of faces. *Oh well, never mind,* I told myself. There were plenty of folks I hadn't seen for a while and with whom I wanted to chat.

I was heading toward a group of people I knew when I spotted John. He was standing alone against a door, holding his newly acquired Dove.

"Congratulations!" I said as I stuck out my hand. "My name's Patti Roberts, and I just want to know how much longer I'm going to have to wait for that lunch date!"

We both laughed. He certainly wasn't put off balance in the least by my impertinent attempt at humor. After talking briefly, I left, thinking that this man was already my friend. It was a nice feeling.

Eventually, my date finished his business and took me home. It *had* been our last date. He did not come in to join the party.

John

I felt a little conspicuous and awkward, standing there holding the award in my hand. I didn't want to appear to be courting congratulations. I very much wanted to be out of there. My parents had come down for the occasion, as had several friends, but we had become separated. So I decided to wait by the door and let them find me. Then I saw her.

Patti was pretty much what I had expected. She came right up to me and introduced herself. I guess that took me back a little. Her dress looked expensive, and her hair was almost too perfect. (At least it wasn't a beehive. I've always found it difficult to talk to a beehive!) She was very easy to talk with, though, and I actually enjoyed it. I decided right then that if she'd still go, a luncheon date would be in order. I was quietly excited about the prospect for two reasons: One, she seemed to be someone I could enjoy being with. Two, I could silence my mother. Seven or eight months ago I had made the mistake of telling her that I had had a nice conversation with Patti on the telephone. Every time I talked with my mother after that she would ask, "Have you called that Roberts girl back yet?" Each time I would tell her that things were busy, and I'd get around to it one of these days.

I got around to it the week after the Dove Awards ceremony. I had a recording session that morning, and we were to have lunch at one o'clock. The session ran a little late so I had to hurry to make our lunch date. As I was going out the door, I noticed that Randy Scruggs, my partner, was leafing through a magazine that had an article about Patti and her girls. "You'd better read this," he said, "so you'll know what you're getting into." He laughed as I took the magazine and quickly scanned the piece.

Patti

Several days after the awards, the phone rang.

"So how about lunch?" It was John. Laughingly I said that I would like that, and we made a date to go to a popular Nashville restaurant.

Something came over me when it was time to get dressed for lunch. *I don't want this person to think I'm impressed,* I said to myself. So I put on blue jeans, a polo work shirt, a straw hat with holes in it (a nicely shaped bowler, nevertheless it did have holes), cowboy boots, and an honorary Palm Springs sheriff's badge that someone had given me. *The badge speaks of power, and the hat speaks of not caring,* I thought. I was going to give this person a lot of mixed messages, to make sure he couldn't typecast me, pigeonhole me and, therefore, gain some leverage to control me—or hurt me.

When I opened the front door after his ring, I was sure that I saw his eyes roll back in his head. That wasn't quite the effect I had anticipated! But the only other time he had seen me, I had looked very much the lady. This time I think I only succeeded in causing a slight wave of amusement. Oh well.

By the time we got to talking, though, I was no longer thinking about mixed messages or power. We conversed like two poets. We exchanged song lyrics and poems. We talked about matters of the heart and of the soul. It was so refreshing as to be intoxicating. My mind raced right along with my pulse as we drifted further and further out on a sea of wonderful thought. Strangely enough, we never once mentioned the music business. We didn't talk about power and prestige or making it to the top of the gospel charts. We didn't even speak of ministry, although we did speak of God.

John was easy to talk to. There was nothing in me that he censured. I think that was the first time that had ever happened to me. I was used to men kind of carving me up into a little image of what they found comfortable. Even in conversations I was used to feeling as though I were being censured, both mentally and emotionally. But between John and me, there was a gliding flow.

Lunch lasted until five o'clock! We had spent all our time having a true and nourishing conversation. It was intense without being depleting. I had the wonderful confidence of not having to think back on what I had said and wishing I had been more careful or less candid. There were no embarrassing memories of having said outrageously stupid things just to keep a conversation moving or avoid a dreaded, awkward silence. John and I had spent those hours talking like real people. When one spoke, the other listened with the heart as well as with the ears.

We were bold enough to speak of past hurts. That is a pretty dangerous thing to talk about on a first date—to be so vulnerable as to say, "I hurt." There was an unspoken invitation that passed between us to lay aside walls and protective mechanisms and pour out what had, in some cases, never been exposed.

Our conversation probably would have gone on into the evening, but John was producing a recording session, so he took me home and left. But the next day he called me. That seemed perfectly logical; I expected that he would. If he had not called me, I think that I would have called him. I didn't think of myself as forward or unusually bold, but I would have called John, because something very important had happened between us, something that should not be allowed to slip out of focus or quietly fade away.

2

The List

What is odd to me, looking back on this sequence of events now, is that I remember clearly not thinking of John in terms of romance. It is odd because, in actual terms of what is authentically romantic, I had just had a most remarkably loving encounter with another human being. I think it was the first such conversation of my life.

But my list of criteria for what I deemed necessary in a husband obscured my vision of who had been placed before me. Somewhere along the way, I read in one of Paul Yonggi Cho's books that one should be quite specific with the explanations of one's needs and desires when petitioning God. I guess you could say that my list of necessary attributes in a husband became something of a prayer list.

I can look back on my list now and be somewhat amused, because it is obvious that I thought more in terms not only of what would look good to my peers, but also of what would most benefit me in my chosen field of ministry.

The man that God was supposed to send me (fulfilling God's end of the bargain, because I had been so specific) was to be (a) successful in his business and at the top of his field—it would be a great benefit to my overall plans if his success translated itself into masses of wealth; (b) physically handsome and fit; (c) not a preacher; (d) socially oriented; (e) supportive of my ministry; (f) loving toward my children, and me, too. . . . The list went on for several more points, containing a bit about personal styles of dress, appreciation of poetry, and the like.

The list served two purposes: one, to alert God to my needs and, two, to remind Him that He had called me to give my talents to Him within the church structure. It was obvious to me that if I were ever going to re-enter evangelical circles after my divorce, I must be equipped with such a mate, a ticket of sorts. It is odd that I thought of a mate as equipment, but considering my past conditioning, I guess that is to be expected.

My choice in dates had tended to reflect this list pretty well.

In the years following the break-up of my marriage, I observed a strange phenomenon in regard to who was and was not acceptable to minister in the circles in which I had previously traveled. Unacceptable would be one who had been caught in some embarrassing public sin, such as murder, tax evasion, embezzlement of church funds, child abuse, and, of course, divorce. If one happened to be the guilty party or, in some cases, the victim of such sins, one could pretty well give up the idea of a public ministry, unless the deeds were done before the profession of faith.

There were loopholes, however, and it was the loopholes that both outraged me and gave me hope. You must remember that I was still struggling with the fear that if I didn't sing or otherwise minister the gospel publicly, I would have thwarted my calling and thus my very purpose for being. I knew that God had placed me in limbo for a while following my divorce, but I still felt that ultimately His desire for me was that I sing, but not in Hollywood or on Broadway or in supper clubs. Yet those would have presented very small obstacles by comparison to the locked front doors of the house of God.

Forgiveness, extended grace, and mercy were loopholes that I found encouraging. It occurred to me that after a period of healing, I would be able to return to my much beloved singing and that I might even have something to share that was born out of failure and the experience of God's cleansing. There were those in the body of Christ who would not allow one of His soldiers simply to expire on the battlefield. They embraced the wounded.

The other reality I thought about was that some of those who control pulpits, airwaves, and religious groupings bend to raw power and obvious wealth. I had seen that if one had some form of clout, one's sins, however shocking, just might be overlooked. I reasoned that this had nothing to do with righteousness and everything to do with reality.

Obviously this is a classic testimony of not trusting God with one's person or ministry. What I was forgetting is that what God calls into being He will in time cause to triumph over any obstacle of any size or shape—including some people within the church.

I guess I should clarify something here. If I had felt that my purpose for having been born was to be a spot welder in Barstow, California, my thought processes to achieve that job would have been the same. What we are talking about here is one woman's fear of having been born to do something and of her being prevented from doing it. I found it unbearable to consider that I might never be able to achieve my essence of being. When I was formed in the mind of God, and then in my mother's womb, God had a distinct and unique reason for breathing life into me. A very real definition of hell, for me, would be to live and die and not experience that reason. This was my fear.

I knew that I could re-enter the ministry if I married rich, or if I married powerful. I could circumvent any judgment made against me from political considerations rather than heart-felt convictions. Yes, I realize now that this is a pitiful rationale, but, unfortunately, it seemed to hold water then.

Thank God I did have the presence of mind enough to understand that meeting John was more than a chance happening. I felt compelled to draw him into my inner circle and to let myself, likewise, be drawn into his. Even at the beginning it would have been unthinkable not to nurture our relationship in whatever form it emerged. So, although John did not have the fame, the fortune, or the social veneer that I wanted in a husband, I agreed to go out with him again.

Our next date was supposed to be a tennis game on a Saturday morning. I can't play tennis very well, but having cute outfits and a desire to be with John, I accepted! Before our tennis game, we were going to have breakfast, so we drove out to a local eatery specializing in country cooking. At noon we were still sitting there talking.

John told me the most incredible things about his life. His conversation hit me at such a deep level that it frightened me. He told me about having become a conscientious objector during the Vietnam war. I'd never heard such an emotional story about convictions and honor as he began to speak.

3

A Bullet

John

There was only one bullet in the gun on that fall Saturday in 1962.

Actually it was a shotgun shell that had been carefully loaded that morning by the man everyone in town knew as Beano. He was the unofficial mascot of our high school basketball team. Although he lived kitty-corner across the street from me, I never knew what he did for a living before he retired. But I can still hear the crowd going crazy as he stood on the gym floor with the cheerleaders and twirled his jacket round and round. "Go, Beano," they'd yell as he swung it all the faster. Other than those few hours on Friday night, all I remember him ever doing was smiling a lot and working on the old black car in his driveway. Except for once.

To this day I don't know why it was Beano who took me hunting for the first time instead of my father. Youngsville was, and still is, in the center of some of the best deer hunting country in Pennsylvania. Dad said that hunters used to come all the way from places like Pittsburgh and Cleveland; hunting was that good. I would always look away when I'd see hunters heading back to the city with trophies tied by all fours across the hoods of the cars. I didn't know the meaning of words like *sanctity* and *conscience* then. I just knew that the sight of dead deer made my stomach feel the same as the time Denny Walton and I snuck down by the Brokenstraw Creek to try smoking a green cigar!

On that Saturday morning, I walked across the street and helped Beano load up the black car. Then off we went. Beano had brown spots on his hands, I remember. The steering wheel was huge and the dash was black enamel with a chrome screen over the radio speaker. How excited I was to be allowed to go with Beano all by myself! This trip would get me ready to go on many future hunting trips with my father.

When I was younger, I watched in wonder as Daddy would get ready for hunting season. He would take the guns down from the shelf in his bedroom closet and clean them. Then he would go somewhere uptown and come back with a very official-looking license that he placed inside a yellow plastic cover and pinned on the back of his red plaid coat. Hunting was a ritual of manhood to me. I couldn't wait until I had my very own license strapped on my back. A hunting trip with Dad wouldn't be the same as the hundreds of times I had roamed the banks of the Brokenstraw with my friends, pointing stick guns. This would be the real thing.

So it was exciting to have this practice run with Beano. That day, we would just be hunting for squirrels; no license was needed. Although I was a little nervous, I felt I could get over that and be ready to get my deer hunting license next month. Dad would be proud.

When we stopped at the edge of the woods and got out of the car, Beano showed me how to hold the shotgun. He told me stories of hunts that his father had taken him on when he was a boy. I wanted my own stories to tell. Finally, convinced that I had a grip on the basics, Beano and I set out for the deep woods.

We walked for nearly an hour before we found the spot Beano wanted. He didn't seem to be in a hurry, so we sat down on a log and had our sandwiches first. While we waited, I felt excited and nervous—even a little scared—at the same time. *Maybe,* I thought, *this is what it feels like to be a man. . . .*

Telling the story for the third time in two days, it seemed as if it were just yesterday that Beano had lightly touched my arm and said, "Shhh, take your time. Wait till you have a clear shot. Squeeze the trigger gently."

"This is all very interesting, Private Thompson, but it doesn't matter if I believe you. You had your chance to file for CO status when you were sworn in. I'm sorry, but I can't recommend this."

I was standing at attention in front of an Army captain, trying to explain to him the beginnings of my beliefs that had led me to apply for conscientious objector status. My hunting story was important, but he wouldn't let me get to the end of it.

The captain closed the folder and handed it back to me.

"Thank you, Sir," I said politely, saluted, and started for the door.

"Thompson," he said. "Good luck with the major."

As I walked back to the barracks, I thought of the interviews ahead—with the major and the lieutenant colonel and the colonel and the general of the post. I didn't know if I could go through with the appeal.

I had received my draft notice earlier that year. I was a full-time staff member for Campus Crusade for Christ, International. My lottery number was thirty-five. At the time, there were about four thousand staff members in our organization, and most of the men had ministerial deferments. But the draft board in Warren, Pennsylvania, had never heard of Campus Crusade, and as far as they were concerned, I was just living in California with all those other crazy people, trying to get out of the war.

I took my Army physical at the induction center in downtown Los Angeles. Up to that point of my life, the people in that building were the worst I had ever seen. The emaciated person who stood directly in front of me in the vision test line made a great show, when his name was called, of reaching into his right eye socket and pulling out a glass eyeball! Those behind me in line were equally original in their defiance.

Two months later, I reported to the airport for my flight to an induction center in Missouri. As we inductees stood in four neat rows after our arrival, preparing to take the oath, a sergeant asked if any of us desired to file for the status of conscientious objector. I had never even considered that as an alternative. No one spoke up. We were sworn in and issued fatigues first. Next we lost all of our hair in about forty-five seconds. Then came our first Army meal and bedtime.

The next morning we were up and halfway through a three-mile run by 5:30 A.M. After lunch, we ran again. This time, a short, heavy-set Jewish kid from New York tripped and fell as we were running. The drill sergeants immediately yelled at him to get up, calling him every name imaginable. He tried to run and fell again. The company ran on. We heard later that day that he had died of a heart attack. Our entire company was shipped out the next morning to Kentucky.

The first two weeks of basic training were fairly tough. In the third week, we began rifle training. The last phase of target training is done with human-shaped targets.

It was then that I began to remember my trip with Beano, and Denny Walton and the cigar. How could I shoot at a human-shaped target, knowing that I was being trained to kill, at another's command, a real, live person?

For a few days, I wrestled with my feelings and prayed as I had never prayed before. *How would this look to the folks back home?* I wondered. I had been a paperboy, a football player, and had run the pro shop at the local ski resort the winters I was in high school. I was just a typical small-town American boy, who had never dreamed I would have to choose such a road. I didn't want to embarrass my parents, and I loved my country. But finally I knew I couldn't go through with the training.

"You what? You candy _____! I can't believe it! You musta been born with a g____d_____ silver spoon in your mouth."

I had no choice but to listen as the drill sergeant yelled obscenities at me in front of two companies of trainees at the weapons range. I had just handed him my rifle, saying, "I can't go on with this target training." He called for another instructor to take me to the company commander's office, where I had to tell the commander the same thing.

The next weeks were worse than I could ever have imagined. The procedure called for me to compile a set of documents from high school teachers, ministers, football coaches, my parents, and anyone else who could substantiate my claim that I, in good conscience, could not kill another person when ordered to. Along with these letters, I had to have personal interviews with every officer, from my company captain to the general of the fort, in my chain of command. They had to recommend or disapprove my application, and their letters became part of my file. Every officer that I met with, except one, recommended that I be given the status of conscientious objector. The one dissenting vote believed that I was sincere, but that I should have filed at the time of my induction.

After my letters and documents had arrived and I had completed all my interviews, I then had to send the complete dossier to the Department of the Army in Washington. The entire process took about six months. With the exception of rifle training, I had to go through two entire rounds of basic training. During this time, the drill sergeants never let up. Often when the rest of the company was in rifle training, I would have to do punishment jobs, such as digging a hole six feet deep and three feet across, then filling it in and moving down three feet to start over. This would go on hour after hour. At other times, I was made to stand in water up to my shoulders and hold a stick (in make-believe rifle fashion) over my head while the rest of the company took weapons training. I had several days of this standing-in-water punishment.

The evenings were my only times alone. I began to spend time reading the Bible and praying. I read Dietrich Bonhoeffer's *Cost of Discipleship* and found it both challenging and sobering. I had never before been in a position of having to trust God. Nor had I ever paid any sort of cost for saying I was following what God would have me do. This was all new, and I was very alone. But I had an inner peace that, for me, this was the course.

My precious great-grandmother Mamie died during these months of waiting. We had always been very close, so her death came as a shock. When the sergeants told me about her death, they laughed. It was touch and go, but finally I was allowed two days' leave for her funeral.

"Get your _____ out of bed!" shouted a harsh voice in my ear. It was 2:30 A.M. The sergeants were laughing again. My application had come back from

Washington the day before—disapproved. The reason stated was: "Applicant appears to be sincere, however, beliefs existed prior to military service. Conscientious Objector status denied." The letter also contained transfer orders for the next day to another military post for advanced infantry training. Although the order had come in early in the day, the sergeants had waited until the middle of the night to tell me. I was on a plane within three hours, no phone calls allowed.

In the new company, I was ordered to begin weapons training. When I asked a military lawyer what my options for refusal were, he informed me that unless I could prove that I had new and pertinent evidence, I would have to take the training and forget the issue or be court-martialed for refusing.

I decided not to take his advice, but to hire a civilian attorney. The entire process that had taken place before would have to be repeated. Again I went through all the interviews, just as before. This time, every officer recommended approval. By now I was nine months into my obligation to the Army. The draft required two years of service.

The company I was assigned to started out treating me the same as did my old company. After the first month, however, they began to respect, if not agree with, my position and the degree of my conviction. Soon, instead of being forced to stand in water up to my shoulders, I was given some administrative duties. Then I was promoted, followed by a second promotion. I even went water skiing with the captain! This time, I was told quietly, in the mess hall, that my grandmother Alta was gone.

About five and a half months into the second application process (eleven and a half months from my induction), the battalion commander called me to his office. He offered to pull my application and assign me to finish my remaining year right where I was. He said that I'd never have to carry a weapon and could continue living off the post. Maybe there'd even be another promotion. If I didn't agree, he said, the odds were that the second application would be disapproved. "In fact," he said, "I've never seen a second application approved. Ever."

"What will happen," I asked, "if it is disapproved?"

"You'll either go through weapons training or spend several years in Leavenworth Penitentiary."

"Thank you for the offer," I told him, "but I have to see it through. I trust God." For the next two weeks I barely slept.

The letter came in the noon mail, and the captain called me in to tell me. I had been approved!

I can't describe my feelings—relief, joy, amazement, fear, thankfulness—all those and more. I knew very little of God's will and obedience. I had been scared and desperate, but He was there where I turned.

It took several days for the paperwork to be completed, but I finally received the orders. They stated that I was recognized as a conscientious objector by the United States government, and I was given a full honorable discharge. I had been in the Army for one year—exactly 365 days!

. . . I tried to steady Beano's huge gun, wondering if I could somehow just put it down instead of firing it. But Beano whispered, "Now," and I pulled the trigger. The gun threw me back a foot for each of my twelve years. All I'd hit was a small squirrel. I told Beano that I didn't even want to carry the shotgun back to the car. He understood.

To my knowledge, my father's guns have stayed in his closet on the back shelf since that day. Hearing of my shock at having killed, Dad retired his guns. We never did go hunting together.

4

Love...It Never Occurred to Me

Patti

ohn sipped his coffee, leaned back in his chair, and breathed a deep sigh. Even though he had couched this bit of personal history in rather poetic and sanitized terms, I, nevertheless, was aware of the bruising and crushing effect those experiences had had on him. I wondered just how he could continue to respect the government for allowing such things to happen. Did he harbor bitterness?

I kept thinking of all the fellows I knew who had simply put in for, and sometimes finagled, ministerial deferments rather than go to Vietnam. I still wonder just how many young men suddenly heard the call of God to the pulpit on the heels of hearing the nightly war reports on the six o'clock news.

Here was a man who could have fled to Canada or pushed hard for a legitimate deferment, since, indeed, he was already in the ministry of Campus Crusade for Christ, International, holding a full-time position with New Folk, Campus Crusade's musical evangelistic arm. Instead, he thought he should go and serve his country. And perhaps he did. Perhaps when men of conviction stand for what they believe to be right, they are indeed serving us all by reinforcing the moral fiber that undergirds any successful society.

I respected John's taking the position that he had, even though my family background espoused different values, and my respect was expensive respect. My father lies in a cemetery in Oregon, his grave marked by a simple stone supplied by the Veteran's Administration. His long imprisonment by the German Army, after he was shot down on a bombing mission during World War II, left him with wounds of body and spirit, from which he never fully recovered. He died when he was only forty-five. Daddy's life had been forever altered by the fact that he had gone to war. I suspected that John's had been altered by the fact that he hadn't.

Here, in front of me, was a man whose idealism was as strong as my own. I wondered why idealism is almost always a sure bet of coming pain of some sort. The lofty idealists of this world seem to court the disfavor of the ruling power structure wherever they find themselves. Now, though, after years of misplaced or mismanaged idealism, I wanted God to temper my idealistic ways and unclothe in me any rebellion against authority that might masquerade as idealism. I wanted my own hot and fervent thoughts of what is right and worthy to be sacrificed, or to be refocused, so that they reflected God's ideas rather than mine.

I had been born in an era and to a generation that thought it would change the world—a child of the flower generation. My own expressions of idealism had drawn me to Oral Roberts University in Tulsa, Oklahoma. I had gone there to give myself to God so that through the education I would receive, and through the ministry of the Roberts family, I might take God's light to dark places and His voice to those who had never before heard His name. It didn't turn out for me quite as I had expected it to. There had been mistakes, disappointments, pain, sin, and finally, the failure of my marriage to Richard Roberts.

I wondered how John handled his idealism in today's world, particularly in the gospel music industry.

After that Saturday breakfast, John and I went out almost every night. It wasn't until a dinner date about two weeks later, however, that John signaled his willingness to hear about my previous marriage. Usually it is a death warrant to a budding relationship ever to discuss one's previous marriage or divorce, but in this case it was important for us both to put as many cards out onto the table as we could bear. We each needed to know just what we were dealing with. Where were the land mines? Where were the snipers?

Until that night, John had shown little or no interest in who I formerly was, the public me. That was odd, because most people I met heavily identified me as being the former Mrs. Richard Roberts. Most people seemed quite unable to accept me in my inauspicious present form. I can't tell you how many conversations with total strangers began with some form of "Ooh, what was it like being . . . " (a) Oral Roberts' daughter-in-law, (b) Richard Roberts' wife, (c) famous, (d) on TV, or something similar.

John wouldn't ask these questions. I assumed it was because he was not only polite, but also sensitive to how I might feel, being positioned and pigeonholed only by my past. Slowly it dawned on me that he simply didn't care much about the past public me. He absorbed and accepted the present me. Maybe that was a little naïve of him, because, like it or not, we bring to the present the distillation of the past—both the good and the bad. Apart from God's healing and forgiving, we are inevitably "what we were."

John's warm-hearted acceptance of me as a woman gave me a curious need to pour out to him my past. And pour I did.

We were dining that particular night at a restaurant with decor reminiscent of World War II. The music of Benny Goodman and Glenn Miller wafts through the air, occasionally interrupted by a radio release telling the news of various battles our boys were fighting. Patriotic posters cover the walls, making the whole place look as if it could have been situated on the edge of some wartime military base.

The hostess seated us in an area that was made to look as if it had been bombed, quite an appropriate setting to be in as I told John of my past marriage and its subsequent demise. Not fearing myself to be on thin ice, I told him of my divorce, of my leaving Tulsa after my former husband remarried, and of my settling in Tennessee.

After ten years of marriage, two beautiful children, and hundreds of television shows, my private world had crumbled. My private, as well as my public, identities were gone along with the marriage. In a brief span of time, I had managed to lose a husband, a job, a home, and a community. Perhaps saddest of all, I had lost my sense of being and purpose. I had left the evangelical empire that swirls around the Roberts family with only my children, a few pieces of furniture, my African violets, and enough money to buy time to start life all over again. I wasn't sure what life was to hold outside of the "magic kingdom" in which I had lived most of my adult life. Yet, surprisingly, I felt protected, loved, and, oddly enough, hopeful. I had no idea who or what I was or if I had any value, but in this massive personal earthquake, I knew that God still loved me. Maybe I would no longer be His bright little television star, maybe I would never again mount a stage and sing of Him, but I felt His love. Still, I could not truthfully tell John that God's love had been enough for me. I had refused to accept it as enough, and that attitude had bred some pretty staggering problems.

I also told John about Daddy, my beautiful father who died in what should have been the bloom of his years. I disclosed as much of my inner feelings as I had dared disclose to myself. Just by being himself, John had offered me the rare opportunity to release a torrent of long pent-up sorrow. But more important, he later proved capable of absorbing a long pent-up store of joy—wonderful waves of life-giving joy.

Over salad and steak, we shared previously locked-up rooms of our hearts. There were moments when we both teared up. At such times, his hand would find its way across the candle-lit table and cover mine. It was warm, steady, friendly. In the whole huge universe, how had I ever been so fortunate to find someone of such fearless capacity for friendship?

We each spoke of our dreams for our children—dreams of wholeness. John and I both desperately wanted our children to grow up without the much-used phrase "broken home" being tattooed on their psyches. My Juli was just seven or eight when she told me that she guessed the divorce was probably the most horrible thing she would ever endure. Christi was sadly withdrawn when the subject of our family break-up was mentioned. John's Matthew and Jessica were finding that an every-other-weekend daddy just wasn't enough. We both yearned for our children to be able to define their homes as "mended homes."

John told me that night about his time with the Evangelical Orthodox Church and what his break with that group of people had cost him: his marriage and his children. He told me that he had been married twice. On the outside, I remained collected and calm, but the news of his two failed marriages startled me. I could understand one marriage failure; I had been there myself and thus could magnanimously grant pardon. But two? I flinched at the thought. One could have been explained away as a mistake of youth. Two—well, that could denote a pattern of failure. Nothing in John's face, though, hinted at anything dark, ragged, and festering beneath the surface. He didn't seem to be running from himself. Yet the number *two* caused little red flags in me to flutter softly.

John told me the painful circumstances that brought about the end of his first marriage. He told me of sin and forgiveness.

Mentally I compared dates. It seems that his world had fallen apart at about the same time mine had, his in Nashville, mine in Tulsa. There were differences in our losses, of course, and they were most evident in our reactions to our marriage failures.

Before his divorce, John had co-produced the song "He's Alive" for a Don Francisco album. The album was a wonderful success, and the success, along with the great way John's other writing and producing had been received, won for him a solid place in the tightly knit community of the gospel music industry. But when his marriage failed, he left all that hard-won success and went into secular music. His rationale was that with sin and failure of such staggering proportions, he could not be hypocritical and stay in gospel music. His life just wasn't exemplary of the gospel.

My reactions were just the opposite. I had tried very hard to remain in gospel music. I wanted to retain my ministry as a gospel singer, and I had tried very hard to "pick myself up, dust myself off, and start all over again." John's understanding of the expectations of a righteous God was more acute than was mine.

John was aware that after repentance must come restoration, and restoration is a process that takes time. I very much wanted to repent, be healed, and hop right back up on the stage. I did not want to admit what I really knew and had seen happen to others: One's healing process is often stunted by the buzz and whir of the daily demands of a public ministry.

Fortunately, I can report that God, in His kind judgments, prevented me from immediately re-entering my ministry. I have come to realize that a marriage failure produces such deep wounds that one must allow them to heal slowly. In this world of immediacy, of drive-through, carry-out everything, there is simply no drive-through, get-it-on-demand healing for such a wound. Forgiveness is instantaneous. Restoration is a process.

I admired John's transparency. To live life with the curtains of one's soul pulled open, with no fear of disclosures, had always been a basic desire of mine—to be that kind of person and to be with people like that. Yet, I held back. With all the fine qualities I was finding in this man, it was a shame that he lacked those other important qualities so necessary for my potential mate. How sad to see all the dearness in this man go to waste! I really needed a husband who would bolster me, if not provide a ticket into the world in which I thought I belonged. With my tainted, scarred reputation, I needed a proper ticket to keep me in the religious world's exclusive blue book.

Yes, I did trust God, that He had called me to be of use to Him. And I knew I ought to be used by Him in the religious system! But I also knew that this is a hard, tough world, and I had better find a way to beat the system if I hoped to be in it. I needed to be in it, because it was the only place where I felt of use; God and I had already been round and round on this subject. I knew that it wasn't His best way, but I was still too damaged and afraid to trust. And waiting on the Lord in order to gain my "wings of eagles" at that time was beyond my grasp of faith.

Then there was the matter of John's having been married twice. The third wife of a man, no matter how repentant, redeemed, and restored that man may be, is rarely a roaring success on the evangelistic circuit. Yet,

I was so warmed by and drawn to this man of basic integrity.

I had lived long enough to know that the world is dotted with hypocrisy and that it isn't uncommon to see things done in the name of God that have nothing to do with God. I knew that some who called themselves to great ministries didn't have anything to do with divine directives. The ministry becomes a fine opportunity to have a meaningful career or to feed one's ego or to seem necessary in a society that desires positions of importance. I knew because I, too, had fed my ego through my public ministry.

So in my damaged, skewed reasoning, I tended to gravitate toward sinners, because I trusted them to be only what they professed to be. At one point, I had written in my diary, "God, give me a redeemed jerk for a husband!" The choice of words, though crude, was purposeful. I had come to a place at which I wanted to see life in absolutes. I wanted to associate with people of absolutes, preferably those who were absolutely good. But when faced with a person who professed godliness, yet retained the curious fascination of finding just how deeply he or she could wade into the mud of life without noticeably soiling his or her robes, I became nauseated. It is unsettling to be with someone who bears the name of *Christian*, yet who has eyes full of lust or a repertoire of dirty jokes or whose God is wealth. Encountering even one or two of that ilk will whet one's appetite to see life in blacks and whites. It is also quite possible that part of my revulsion came from hating the gray areas in my own life. The ambiguity of grays is damaging to one's spirit. Little white sins turn one's white robes to sleezy tunics, worn ultimately by the crowd known as "lukewarms."

It wasn't that I wanted my future husband to actually be a jerk. I wanted him to be a Christian, but I wanted him to know whence he had come. I wanted him to know and identify his roots and to say out front, "This is what I was. I make no effort to deny it. I am now changed, different." But I didn't want him to hide from his humanity, from the darkness that is in every one of us until we nail it to the cross. Cloaking darkness is so prevalent. Those who come near to such a thing are inevitably bruised, compromised, and crushed in spirit. I knew about bruises. I feared them. So, in my ignorance, I asked God to just send me "a redeemed jerk." I could not stand the thought of a faker. I didn't care what his past was, as long as he owned up to it, yet thoroughly turned from it. I was reaching for a reality of personhood that I knew was rare.

Now, sitting here before me was a man who was owning up to his past, exposing his weaknesses without resorting to the maudlin displays that sometimes come with self-disclosure. Nothing was said for effect, manipulation, or shock value. Best of all he was not a sinner (at least he had no flagrant sins) and was decidedly not a jerk.

That John would tell me things that were both good and bad about his life profoundly affected me. The effect went further than my emotions. I had the ability, in my emotions, to be in love every other week with someone new, because love is so much fun. But this was different. I didn't particularly want to love John. I still didn't like the way he dressed or the car he drove. In fact, there were several things I didn't like about him. Plus, he wasn't rich, famous, or powerful. And I found that to be of the utmost inconvenience.

But there was something so strong in the communication that flowed between us. I didn't know that I was experiencing the basis of a true relationship and true love. The trappings were still so important to me, necessary to my well-being—or so I thought. It never occurred to me that I might be falling in love.

5

Opening Up

Patti

*F*ranklin, Tennessee, is one of the most pictur-esque little towns in America. The Civil War architecture of the buildings is so well pre-served that it gives one a feeling of being lost in time. Movie makers have discovered this fact. It is now quite common to see a mobile filming unit sitting on the square, with directors, stars, and crews bustling about. The townsfolk yawn and go on about their daily routines.

There are visionaries in our community who have invested small fortunes in buying up crumbling buildings of historic importance and completely restoring them to their former stately condition. Ed Stolman, an independent businessman, is one of such. His love affair with Franklin is well documented by the time and creativity he has poured into Main Street, landscaping the area to create a ribbon that runs through the center of town, lined with flower boxes, potted trees, romantic street lights, and colorful awnings that jut out from the building faces like eyelashes on a beautiful woman. Storefront windows display antique jewels, Steuben crystal, one-of-a-kind art pieces, funky clothing, and a mouth-watering assortment of fine foods. There are places like Merridee's Breadbasket on Fourth Avenue, where one can get perhaps the finest pecan cinnamon rolls on the planet. Tom and Merridee McCrea and their fine staff of bakers have added untold tons to the local townsfolk. If I am within a block of Merridee's and the wind is just right, the tantalizing aroma of baking bread guides me like radar into the old converted feed store, whose rafters are heavy with handwoven country baskets awaiting Merridee's offerings. Lucky is the friend who gets a bread basket from Merridee's.

On Saturday morning it often seems that half the town gathers at the bakery to sip a cup of sturdy coffee, read the paper, and consume a couple of thousand calories of Merridee's goodies. Lori's Book and Card Shoppe is on the same street. One can browse for hours up and down the book-lined aisles. Like the bakery, this shop has its own inviting smell. The aroma of thousands of books, cards, calendars, and magazines can be nearly as intoxicating as that of the pecan rolls. It is a deeply satisfying experience to take one's newly purchased book and a cup of coffee to the courtyard that skirts the rear of several of the downtown shops. There on a spring day one can sit in this tiny jewel of a park and while away the hours reading or chatting with the locals, all of whom seem to have something newsy or juicy to share. This is, after all, a small town.

Franklin is a town that begs one to take to the streets and do errands by foot rather than by car. Even tourists have a printed brochure called *The Walking Tour*. People in love are compelled to walk the time-worn sidewalks and share their secrets with each other. John and I were quite suddenly entering the latter category. Occasionally, we would wind up at Dotson's, the wonderful old place next to Earl's the greengrocer. Here was bolstered our strength in order

to keep on talking. Turnip greens and cornbread, cat-
fish and hush puppies, meatloaf and bacon-seasoned
green beans, and an assortment of freshly baked pies
can surely spur one on in the quest for the essence of
another's heart.

John

The waitress at Dotson's filled my coffee cup
again. I don't remember how many times she had done
so, but I did notice that the table next to us had gone
through two sets of breakfast eaters and that mimeo-
graphed luncheon menus were being placed between
the catsup bottles and chrome napkin holders. I was
just getting comfortable. For me this was quite a
departure from the normal. First of all, I don't like to
talk at length about myself. Second, I really didn't
know her that well yet, but I had just told her a story I
had entrusted to only a handful of my closest friends
and family. To my surprise, she actually seemed to be
listening to what I said. I guess I felt safe. Even more to
my surprise, I heard myself, almost as a third person,
telling her the real places in which my heart had been.

I told her about my family. My older sister, Carol, is
a gifted music arranger who began her career as a
pianist at my expense—as a child she always practiced
her piano lessons after the evening meal, while I was
expected to help with the dishes! My brother, Brian, is
a young artist full of talent and hope. I knew through
the lives of my parents that family was a permanent
thing. They were always there. Feeling loved was
something I simply took for granted.

I knew very little of broken families as a young man.
My grandmother Alta (mother's mother) had been
divorced before I was born, but we never talked about it.
It seemed some distant event that didn't touch me.

Another, even further-away mystery was the story of my father's father. Dad grew up in a family of eight—his parents, two sisters, an older and a younger brother, and an identical twin. When Dad was six, his father went to work one day, as usual, on the railroad. It was a payday, which came once a month. He never came home. Ever. Through the years, his family tried to find a trace of my grandfather, but nothing was ever found. To me it was more of a story to tell over coffee, like now, than a broken link in my past. Those two events, the divorce and the disappearance, were the only mysteries that our family seemed to have. Telling Patti about them somehow felt good to me. I thought I'd found a friend.

Grandmother Alta remarried before I was born, and her husband was the only grandfather I knew. When he died (I was ten), I was given a guitar that had belonged to him, and I have had calluses on my fingers ever since. Throughout high school, I played in a rock band. Then I met Gary Powell. He was a few years older than I and traveled in a motorhome, singing in churches. That intrigued me. He was using music to make a statement of his faith in God. He offered me a chance to play with his group, and I took it. I was still in school, but I went with him on several weekend trips. When I graduated from high school, I auditioned for and was accepted as a member of the international cast of Up with People, a touring musical group begun by Moral Rearmament. For a small-town boy, the chance to travel all over the world and perform was intoxicating.

It didn't take a year, however, for me to realize that Up with People was not the place for me. I resigned and headed for California to try to make it in the music business. My family's closest friends in Pennsylvania, Bill and Gladys Meleen, had moved to the Los Angeles area, and they offered me a place to stay. I lived with them for a few weeks, but then I felt it was time to try it on my own. I asked Gladys, who was like my second mother, to take me to the downtown YMCA. She was not too excited, but reluctantly agreed, and I found myself with one suitcase and a guitar standing on a street corner millions of miles from Youngsville.

I wasn't prepared for the scene that awaited me inside the Y. It was like a set from an old film. There were men sitting in the hallways with their knees up to their chins, hiding faces I knew were looking at me as I tried to find a room number that matched the one on my key. Cigarette butts and brown paper bags in the shape of bottles littered the floor. Even the air was heavy. Everything appeared to be in black and white. When I finally reached my room, I was relieved to close the door safely behind me.

I described for Patti the once-green paint that had peeled from the walls and the single, stained sink against one wall. The rest of the bathroom was down the hall. The bed had a mattress not much thicker than the Gideon Bible on the window sill. As I looked out the window, I could have sworn that the men in the hallway had moved out to the sidewalks across the street; there, visible in the flashes of neon light, I could see them in the exact same positions they had held just minutes before. I was frightened on top and excited underneath. It was as if I were trying to force myself into a change in my life that would bring some fulfillment to ease the restlessness I had been feeling recently.

I remember praying for guidance. I sincerely sought to know what I should do next. God, to me, was very personal. I knew that He had something in the midst of all this that would be His purpose for me. Then I remembered a concert that I had attended with my father over a year earlier. The singer was Doug Oldham, and after the concert he told me of a music group called The New Folk, sponsored by Campus Crusade for Christ, International, headquartered in San Bernardino, California.

At about seven o'clock that evening, I used the pay phone in the lobby of the YMCA to call Campus Crusade and eventually made arrangements to be picked up by a man who worked with the organization. The next morning, I waited by the street with my suitcase and guitar. Russ Knipp, a world champion weight lifter who was part of the athletic ministry located at the UCLA campus, came by and took me to a meeting at one of the athletic fraternity houses. Later that day we went on to San Bernardino. During the months I waited for a chance to audition for The New Folk group, I stayed at Campus Crusade headquarters and worked in the bookstore. Eventually I was selected and joined the group.

It was there that I met Kathleen McEver, who also sang in The New Folk. After our first year of traveling, we were married. At that point, I felt as if my life was being pretty well laid out before me. I believed that my music was to be a ministry, not in the traditional sense, but nonetheless a ministry. However, just a month after Kathleen and I were married, I was drafted into the army. After my successful application for conscientious objector status, I rejoined Campus Crusade. In 1972, the year after my honorable discharge from the army, Matthew was born. He was the joy of my life. Precious Jessica Mamie came four years later, another great joy.

At a small table in Dotson's restaurant, a decade later, I was beginning to feel alive. Patti asked me several questions to help her understand the chronology of my stories. I found that her questions came from genuine care. I couldn't believe how easy it was to talk to her and to tell her things no one else knew. I talked without reservation of the joys, the hurts, and the injustices inflicted both on me and by me. I wanted her to know how much I felt responsible for the failure of that marriage. I wanted her to know of the open wound inside me that the divorce had caused by separating me from my children. Even in the telling, I felt a tremendous weight being lifted. Patti understood the things of which I spoke.

6

Grocery Store Roses

Patti

*W*e were taking the first tentative steps of a dance. The movement was unlike anything I had known before. I was at once drawn to and repelled by John, drawn as if by magnets to the heart of this man whom I had known so briefly, and repelled by both the fear of being so inextricably drawn and his exterior circumstances. This quiet man was offering me the next dance . . . and perhaps many following.

A wellspring of communication flowed between us, sweet melodies of knowing, not only a new and fresh depth of sharing, but also a new language, it seemed, unique to us, unguarded, unhampered, and totally without judgment. How wonderful to have such a friend!

Good communication is the basis of relationships, we hear. But it is not just being able to talk to a person that constitutes a good relationship. What happens at the nonverbal level is the telling point. It is what rolls uncensured from the other person's soul to your soul; we were experiencing this. I also began to understand that oneness happens at a soul level, if it ever happens at all. Perhaps this is what Scripture means when it says, "What therefore God has joined together, let not man put asunder" (Mark 10:9). If ever there is a real marriage between two people it probably occurs with the merging of their spirits before it is formalized by religious or civil ceremonies. When I met John, gates began to unlock and open within me, quite apart from my having given conscious consent.

Even though I didn't identify this as a romantic relationship, because John didn't fit the profile of my list, I knew that I longed to be with him. So we dated frequently. Finally, though, I began to feel that he had a romantic interest in me. That frightened me, because it took me to a different level of responsibility.

He's such a wonderful person, I thought. *I don't want him to love me, because he'll never understand that I can never marry him, even though he has a house in Belle Meade and probably is a Republican!* He had no goals to be the most flashy, dashy, cashy guy, which was the kind of man I was hoping for. He didn't have that in him. John's eyes were set on a goal that my eyes couldn't see. I was looking for a form of security and protection. I thought of people who had hurt me or not accepted me, and knew I couldn't live without some kind of protection. But John offered no protection. He offered integrity, love, communion—but not those other things. So I couldn't think of him in terms of love or marriage.

Though John never pushed or came on too strong, because that's not his way, he let me know that he cared for me as more than a friend. I didn't want to hurt this wonderful person, so I began to retreat. He would set up a date, and I would agree to it, but three hours before the date, I'd call and say, "I have a child who has some dreaded malady—I just can't come." What was so awful was that he patiently understood. He didn't protest or condemn me for standing him up. Instead he'd ask if there were anything he could do.

"No, no, nothing, nothing," I'd say. "I'm sure she'll be fine." Then I'd slap on the charm, throw in a few *dears* and *darlings*, pull out all my old schtick, and just tap-dance my way off the phone. But a couple of hours later, he would phone back and say, "You're afraid of something, aren't you?"

After an embarrassing pause I would have to say, "Yes, I really am."

"What's there to be afraid of?"

"I think you like me in a way that I don't like you."

"I think we have such a rapport, that you really don't need to worry about that. Just let me worry. You don't have to bear the weight of my feelings."

He would be so kind, so engaging, that I'd remember all the nice things about our relationship—things that weren't at all romantic in my mind—and I'd invite him over.

When he came to the house, he always brought treats for the girls. They were completely won over. "Mama," they'd say, "don't let this one out the door!" They had seen a few of my dates walk right past them, or pretend to be nice to them only to stay in my good graces, or purely for their own ego's sake, not because they enjoyed or loved the children. The girls could always tell who was interested in them personally. John was, because he loved children.

"Well," I'd say, "when I marry it will be because I'm in love and cannot see life as complete apart from that man. I just don't love John. I like him. I enjoy him. I want to be with him, but I don't love him. I just don't love him."

"Mother," they'd say, "*make* yourself!"

But I couldn't. Relationships were merely to be fun. I was still too damaged, bruised, to know myself or what I needed or wanted in a serious relationship. John's getting serious meant that I had to put the brakes on. I'd go out with him just one more time, and then I'd tell him that was the end. A dinner party at Michael and Susan Card's would be our last date, I decided.

At the Cards' house, we sat in the living room while the other guests played video games, talked, or helped prepare spaghetti. I didn't have much to say to John, and he didn't have much to say to me. I listened to the conversations around us, all the while thinking, *I don't want to be here. I'm uncomfortable and frightened. I've backed myself into a corner again. What am I going to do? I wish this evening would end.*

Then I turned to look at John, this man who was making me so uncomfortable. He was sitting beside me on the sofa, looking straight ahead. At that moment he turned to look at me, and I looked into his eyes. It wasn't a romantic look. I didn't want to appear rude, just friendly. But something happened that I wish someone could explain to me. I don't know what you call it, but something jumped out of the very bottom of my stomach and went through my eyes—not through my brain, it did not ask permission to leave—to John. I felt as though I had been opened up, almost like I had flashed him at a soul level. I was so embarrassed that I turned quickly away.

He grabbed my arm, tugged at it, and said, "Why did you look at me like that?"

"I don't know what you're talking about," I said. "I didn't particularly look at you."

"Yes, you did."

"Well, you must be making that up! I don't know what you're thinking, but I didn't look at you." We were like two little kids quarreling. I can remember my brothers in the back seat of the car fighting and yelling, "Mother, make him stop looking at me!"

Though I tried to pass the incident off with a "you're being silly," in reality I was so stunned I didn't know what to do or say. For the next ten or fifteen minutes, I sat there wondering what had happened. Why had it happened? Whatever it was was not associated with my feelings or my emotions.

My emotions have always preceded everything in my life, which has been a great detriment and stumbling block and has hurt me numerous times. My emotions have been my ruling factor. Even though I love Jesus and want to make Him proud, I have directed my life more by emotion than by conviction and have borne the consequences more times than I can possibly recount. But this look, this communication, by-passed my emotions, and I had no way of recognizing what it might be. To this day, I don't know what to call it. The only thing I can liken it to is the experience of Jesus when, in a large crowd, the lady with the issue of blood touched the hem of His garment. With her touch, He felt something going out of Him. For Him, it was healing power that flowed into the woman's life and body. For me, an essence was exchanged. Something of me went to John, apart from my conscious permission. Yes, obviously, from the very core of my being I was looking for my mate; part of my soul entered his soul.

Somehow I managed to get through the dinner, but underneath the conversation I was horrified at what had happened. My criteria list was still very important to me. I still wanted a ticket back into the religious world. So as soon as we could after the meal, I told John I wanted to leave.

"It's such a lovely evening," John said as we drove back to my house, "and it's still early. I'd love to drive in to Nashville."

"I don't believe I can," I told him.

"It would be nice to go walking in Centennial Park."

Walks in parks just aren't me, and I had no intention of being romantic with him, particularly not in a park. One of my rules in playing the game of love

had, unfortunately, always been: "When in doubt, lie."
At one point in my life, I had been such a serious
woman. So serious about God, so serious about things
of the Spirit. But in human relationships I was just a
flake! I mostly tap-danced my way through encounters
as fast as I could get through them and out the other
door. So I told John, "I can't go walking in the park in
these shoes, so why don't we stop by my house, and let
me pick up some tennis shoes."

When we got to the house, I ran upstairs thinking,
What can I bargain with? I had no intention of getting
my shoes or driving in to Nashville. Then I saw the
manuscript of *Ashes to Gold.* The book was just going
to press at that time. All of my close friends, as well as
my boyfriends (telephone boyfriends, I called them; we
had romantic talks on the phone that had nothing to do
with anything, but were just playing so that everybody
could stay in practice), had read the manuscript. John
had heard about it, but I wouldn't let him read it,
because it seemed as though he would *really* read it.
He would look into me, and I didn't want that. He had
asked several times to read it, but I had always put him
off by saying, "It's being edited."

Aha, I thought, *I'll send him home with the
manuscript. Surely he won't want to walk in the park
when he can read the book.*

I came downstairs without changing shoes. I
didn't even pick up another pair. "I've got a deal for
you," I told John and handed him the manuscript.
"How about if, instead of going to Nashville, we just go
down to Shoney's for a cup of coffee? You've been
saying you want to read my book. Well, if you want to
read it tonight, you're welcome to it. Here it is." Lines
like that had always worked before.

"Thank you," John said. "That's real sweet."

Out of one side of my mouth I'm saying, "Whew!"
and out of the other I'm saying, "Sucker!"

We got back into the car to go for coffee, but we passed Shoney's and before I could say anything, John had turned onto the freeway going north to Nashville.

"There's one thing you ought to know," he said. "You are not going to manipulate me; I'm not the kind of guy who likes it. You didn't go upstairs to change shoes. You went up to find a way to get out of walking in the park. If you want to get your shoes dirty in the mud, that's your problem. I am not going to read your manuscript tonight. We are going to walk in the park!"

I'd been had! Bettered, if you will. I had no choice at that point but to go to the park. I guess I could have demanded to be taken home, but with the steel-willed resolve that sat behind the steering wheel, I am sure I would have been politely, but firmly, let off on the side of the freeway to find my own way home! That idea held no appeal.

Centennial Park was created for Nashville's centennial celebration in 1897. It's a lovely expanse of trees, shrubs, and ponds, surrounding a full-sized replica of the Parthenon of Athens, before war and the elements eroded it. It's an imposing and beautiful building. In the park we walked and talked—as lovers often do, only as far as I was concerned, we weren't lovers. Parks and moonlit walks should be reserved for those fortunate folk who can walk through wet grass and mud, shiver in the early spring air that hasn't lost the bite of winter, and gaze into each other's eyes without taking notice of the elements.

I *was* noticing all of these things, but I mostly noticed that I had been outmanipulated. If I had had a mirror to look into, I'm sure I would have seen egg on my face. It was a sickening feeling.

When I came to, John was telling me about his boyhood and growing up by Brokenstraw Creek in Youngsville, Pennsylvania. He was obviously having a good time. That embarrassed me. Again I felt somehow responsible—his emotions were so tender. My heart was being rubbed raw.

Then John began to tell me about his daughter Jessica. They had spent her birthday right here in this park on the huge stone steps of the Parthenon, under its brilliant floodlights. It was Jessica's sixth birthday, and John alluded to it as though not only was it a very special occasion, but that this cold stone structure also held a very special meaning for him, because they had shared the occasion here.

A kind of sadness floated across his face, and he abruptly ended his narrative without really finishing the story. I guess that whatever he wanted to share with me would have to wait until another time. Apparently it was too tender, too close to the center of his survival mechanism to share with someone who had come reluctantly to this cherished spot.

I felt odd with John that night, as though I were outside myself, watching the scene. John seemed to be posing an unspoken question to me: "Do you like me?" or, worse yet, "Could you love me?" Something in his mannerisms and looks clearly said, *I need you to love me.*

The thought made me shiver. It was so naked, stark, too present. He made no effort to provide me, or himself, with some face-saving emotional back door in case my feelings were not as his. I hated the fact that he was emotionally uninsured. He was disturbingly daring and sincere.

This was such a departure from the type of male-female encounter I was accustomed to. I guess I was used to a lot more fanfare and a lot less substance. Yet, though John was making me very uncomfortable, he was nonetheless engaging.

At the end of our little walk around the park, he turned to me and said, "Would you hug me?"

How embarrassing, I thought. If he had just forced the moment . . . just scooped me up in some big romantic gesture, at least I could have played along. But I couldn't play along here, because he wasn't playing. Nevertheless, I hugged him tentatively.

"Could you be a little warmer?" he asked.

"Well, all right."

But I didn't want to open up those floodgates of whatever was inside me. I didn't want to touch him, didn't want to hold his hand, didn't want to hug him, certainly didn't want to kiss him, had not kissed him, and had no intentions of ever kissing him.

But I hugged John and he hugged me back. *If I can just live through this hug and get in that car and go home, I'll be all right,* I thought. *If I just never have to see him again.* Something very raw and vulnerable in me was being uncovered by his sincerity. Through our interaction, walls were falling down that I had hidden behind for years. They were not only walls that kept me from intimacy, but they were also instruments of safety. I didn't know what to do without them. Yet for years I had prayed that God would knock down these walls, that He would do something to set me free. I wrote poems about being imprisoned in a cell of loneliness and alienation. I pictured myself wild-eyed, hair matted, in tattered rags waiting for years at the bottom of some dungeon floor for the door to open, and the doors never opened. In my poems I would declare that some day, someone would throw open the doors and scoop me up, and he wouldn't mind that my hair was dirty and that I'd been in a dungeon for all those years. He would hold me. Now, here this someone was. I could hear the footsteps coming down the dungeon steps. And I said, *No, no! I like the dungeon!* I had begged God to please set me free. Please let me know a real relationship. But now I prayed, "Oh God, help me learn to love the dungeon." The reality terrified me.

After that night I was even more determined never to go out with John again, no matter what. Yet we continued our wonderful conversations by phone. (As long as we were on the phone, I felt safe, just so I didn't have to see him.) During every break that he had throughout the day, he would call and we would have wonderfully long, enjoyable, rich conversations. We'd talk about our children, about our pasts, and about the dreams we had. Every good thing we'd ever wanted to talk about, we managed to say.

One night he called me very late. Again, we had a delightful talk. Then he said, "My car is in the shop, and I want to have coffee with you at six tomorrow morning."

Now, it was grief to me to get out of bed and get the children to school by eight. In fact, I don't think I even did that; we had a nanny at this time who got the girls off to school. But to placate John, I said I guessed I could do it.

"Would you pick me up at my house?" he asked. "Then we'll go and have breakfast. You can drop me off at the studio after that and go on about your day."

That seemed reasonable, safe enough, until 5:30 the next morning when I thought, *I can't go. Going to someone's house to pick him up for breakfast smacks of commitment to me. I can't do it.*

So I called him and said, "I don't think I can do it. I have a headache and I don't think I can get out of bed. I can't come and get you, and I can't have coffee with you."

"OK," was all he said in reply. Some hours later, though, he called me back. "Do you know that I borrowed a friend's car and went out at four this morning and searched every Kroger in town to find Sonia roses for you? I had them at the house this morning." (Sonias are my favorite.)

Four A.M.! And going to Kroger to find roses! I had

never heard of anybody doing anything like that. It was so sweet; it crushed me—so unbearably, embarrassingly sweet. It was awful. *I don't know if I can bear the pain of someone's doing that,* I thought, *and then having the courage to tell me he had done it!*

His action was so touching, so sweet, it jerked me back to reality, jerked me awake. *Dear God in heaven,* I thought, *who is this person?*

After that, John asked me out one more time. "It's Thursday now. I have to go up to Ohio, but I'll be back Sunday. We'll go out Sunday night." Again I didn't stick to my resolution, but agreed to go. I really thought I could do it this time. But Sunday rolled around, and at about 4:30 I called him to say that I just couldn't go. Again, he was understanding. And again he called back later and we talked about my being afraid of a relationship. He was so kind and so genuinely interested in why I was afraid of relationships that I couldn't stand it, and again I invited him over.

He came with Baskin Robbins chocolate mint ice cream—which happens to be a favorite of us all. He fed the children theirs in big bowls in the kitchen. I felt out of control—and I didn't like the feeling. In all my other relationships, if I couldn't have some element of control, or at least know what was going on, I got out. But this one I could neither control nor get out of. I had prayed for that kind of relationship. I had prayed that that kind of healing would come into my life, that I would somehow grow beyond the need to control. But now that it was here, it was really frightening.

We went into the den, which at that time didn't have any furniture except a stereo, which was playing a lovely waltz. We began to dance. It was better than talking, better than having to deal with anything. As we waltzed, there was such a stillness and calm that I began to cry—something I never did with men. I was embarrassed, but I couldn't help myself.

"What's wrong?" John asked.

"I don't know," I sobbed. But I did know. I thought I heard God speak to me about John, and I wasn't tuned in to listen. I didn't want to hear. But there was a sweet, sweet assurance that my husband was dancing with me. That was what made me cry, not that at last Mr. Right had come. Rather I was saying, *O God! This is not a ticket! This may be love, this may be reality, but it is not a ticket into the religious world. And how will I survive in a ticket world with no ticket? Lord, you know I expected you to bring me a ticket. Don't you care about my calling, my work, my destiny?*

But, of course, the Lord cared about my heart, about my life, about my feelings, about my children, even about my career. But not about my ticket! It was I who cared about the ticket.

I cried so hard that I thought I would collapse. I knew that what I was hearing was right; there was such a deep, sweet peace to it. But, oh, all those preconceived ideas and desires I knew I would never have. I wouldn't buy my way into the ministry. I wouldn't win over the people who had hurt or shunned me. I wouldn't beat them at their own game, and I couldn't bear it. It hurt so bad.

That God did all this in the name of love devastated me. That's the most outrageous act that God has ever performed in my life. It left me completely without control. I was so frightened. Suddenly I was alone because of *not* being alone—I was nurtured and protected and cared for and loved, but in none of the ways that I had planned. To be stripped of the protection *I* wanted hurt. And what frightened me even more was that my ability and desire to control seemed to be draining out of me without my permission.

7

Face to Face

Patti

can look back now and see that God was beginning a healing in me at a very deep level. But people ought to know that sometimes healing can be terrifying, and obviously that's why a lot of us don't choose it. It must have been that God had heard my heart's cry for release; He by-passed my brain chatter and listened to my heart.

That evening I cried so hard that we had to go in to the living room and sit down. John held me on his lap, patted me, and then began to rock me. Of course, that made me cry even harder. I cried for three or four hours, until I had no more tears.

I saw myself as a tree, part alive and part dead, some branches blooming and beautiful, some dead. The image formed in my mind as we were waltzing. I could see and feel those dead branches falling off. I could almost hear them crashing at my feet. Each time another branch fell, I would cry harder: *I don't want it to fall off!* Each branch was something I had held onto, a way I could be my own god, a way I wouldn't have to trust, a way of not going through the black night of the soul with just my hand in God's. *I have had all of that kind of walk I can bear,* I thought, so I was going to prop myself up with all those other things. But God said, "No, you're not." So all those dead limbs came crashing down around me.

By the end of the evening, I could face the fact that I really loved this person. Love was doing this, not need, not manipulation. It wasn't a business move. It was only love. And love stood there naked as a jaybird! Love stood there as what it is—costly, frightening, wonderful, peaceful. I had never seen love before.

I knew now that I really loved John. Of course, I couldn't tell him that, because I'd spent those weeks denying that I cared very much. I couldn't even deal with the truth myself. But the next time he asked me out, I didn't turn him down. I didn't even bother to try. We went out to eat, then he took me to his house. The roses he had bought for me were still sitting on his dining room table, petrified as an everlasting reminder of my jerkiness! We talked and laughed and he played his guitar. Then he started kissing me. We'd both had a lot of garlic, but my motto is: If you really love someone, why not enjoy that garlic! If there's freedom there's freedom!

John had never kissed me before, and I had wondered if there was any real passion in our relationship. But I need not have wondered. There was such a burst of life, of joy, when he kissed me that I pushed him away, slid off the sofa onto the floor and kicked my feet! "Don't touch me," I squealed. "I think I'm having a heart attack! Give me a minute to catch my breath."

I had spent so many years in a dead relationship in which there wasn't that spark of wonder, so many years tap-dancing and pussyfooting around in a world in which kissing is like hand-shaking. Suddenly something was decidedly different, so incredibly beautiful. I guess this is what they make movies about!

When I caught my breath, we laughed and kissed and talked and drank out of the big cup of life. It was a banquet. John pulled back for a minute, looked at me and said, "I love you."

Then he was embarrassed, because he had decided not to tell me he loved me; that would give me too much control. But that was all right, because I already knew he loved me. But I did appreciate getting back at least this much of a button to push. *Aha!* I thought. *I've got one on him, because I have no intention of saying I love him, even though I do love him and will always love him and can't help but love him and choose to love him.* But I didn't say that to him.

The next night we went out again. In the car we kissed and hugged and laughed and enjoyed each other. "You know," I said, "I never dreamed that I would be in love with somebody in the music business." And then, of course, he laughed at me! We had both disclosed our hearts without planning to—which was just as well. Now it was all out in the open. There we were, in love! And happy with the fact that we were in love.

By this time, all of my circle of friends thought I was nuts. We had all planned on my marrying a charismatic "Prince Rainier" type—a wild mixture of spirituality, cosmic googah, and tremendous wealth, . . . a social butterfly. My pals liked the men I had previously dated. We went to and gave great parties. There were always people of power and wealth around. But John was not into that at all, could not care less. As far as tending the social circuit, he displayed no interest.

My friends were also more than a little concerned that I might be rushing into something without thought. They loved me and my children and didn't want to see us caught up in a whirlwind romance that might have a regrettable outcome.

My friends even went so far as to intimate that they expected something different from me. They couldn't or wouldn't see what John was, and I couldn't explain to them what he was. I couldn't explain that, though I was sorry they objected, my heart had found a home; it was like comparing apples and oranges. They didn't seem to have a basket at that point to put my explanation in. In all fairness to them, three months earlier, I wouldn't have had one either. I didn't know then about this depth of relationship, and even now I simply couldn't explain what had happened to me.

One night we had gone out to eat with some of John's friends. During the evening, I suddenly thought of something. "You know, John, Tommy Tyson is coming to town. He could marry us."

We all laughed, and I realized what I had done. "I can't believe it," I said. "I think I just asked you to marry me. Excuse me, I'm so sorry!"

But John just said, "OK, why don't you tell me about Tommy Tyson? Maybe he *could* marry us."

Tommy Tyson, my friend and father figure for over twenty years, was and is one of this nation's greatest evangelists. I had always wanted him to perform the wedding ceremony should I ever remarry.

After all that crying in my living room that night, marrying John was just a given fact. Why would I marry anyone else? What could we possibly do but marry each other? I used to say to him, "I know that when they close the lid on my casket, you'll be there. And should you precede me, I'll be the one standing there when they close the lid on you." I knew that. Whatever had happened, I knew it was a bonding so good, so right, so nurturing and life-giving and healing, that I couldn't deny it. I shouldn't deny it. To deny it would be to deny everything that's real, that's precious, that's of God.

Later that evening, when John brought me home, he said, "Since you brought it up, would you marry me?"

"Of course," I said.

We decided, however, that however much I wanted Tommy Tyson to marry us, the fact that he was going to be in Nashville in May, just a week or two away, made it impossible. We couldn't get our plans together by then. We'd only met in April! We set a date in the middle of June.

Though there was no way we could deny the relationship, there was something we were overlooking. I, particularly, should have thought of it. My book *Ashes to Gold* was just about to be published, in which I talked a great deal about how important it is to get counseling and to take your relationships to God. Obviously, I had been burned by following my emotions—and sometimes my intellect—into a relationship. I knew that people needed more than that. When I thought about it, I knew that John and I probably needed more than our emotions to go on in a marriage.

But the deep abiding love that was flowing between us far outweighed any questions that flitted by now and then. There were some things about John that I wondered about, some areas of his life I wasn't really sure of. But I pushed aside all these "gray areas" for the moment to leave room for soaking up the happiness I had so longed to feel. My weary, wandering feet had found the cool, lush meadows of love. After thirty-five years of half life, I was born into life as it was meant to be experienced.

8

Beginning Again

Patti

Theologically, there are many ways we can argue second marriages. But if the peace of the Lord means anything, I surely felt it about the beginning of this marriage.

We can look back to times in our lives when we have heard God or have felt His presence and pleasure in an unmistakable way. The experience becomes a monument, something of a surety to remember in times of uncertainty, confusion, or fear. It is an Ebenezer, a marker along the way (I Samuel 7:12). For both John and me, our wedding was such an event. In the bad times that came for us later on, we both looked back at our wedding to the light we saw on that day and the memory of touching God. It was a certitude, something sure and steadfast. When we felt ourselves falling into emotional quicksand, we could remember the solidity we touched on that day, the reality, and knew somehow that it was still a part of us. If I had not had such a powerful experience on my wedding day, I don't know whether I would have had the faith to hang on when the walls and roof caved in on our relationship.

For both of us on our wedding day, the peace of God was so powerful as to be tangible. And the joy of the day was intoxicating. Many times we have joyous moments, but they are a mixture of joy and anxiety, or joy and something else. June 19, 1983, was for me a day of unalloyed peace and happiness.

We chose to be married on a Sunday afternoon in the United Methodist church the girls and I had been attending since we moved to Franklin. Our families and our dearest friends were there to share our happiness with us, and we all went to church together in the morning. John's parents had driven down from Pennsylvania, and my mother and step-father flew in from Oregon. My older brother couldn't come, but my younger brother gave me away. John's sister played the organ.

The four children were the wedding party. Jessica, Juli, and Christi wore ivory gowns of dull satin peau de soie trimmed in lots of creamy lace. Their long hair was braided with baby's breath and Sonia roses. They carried nosegays of Queen Anne's lace (I know it's a weed, but I adore it), Sonia roses, and white lilies in square holders of cream moiré edged with lace and tied with pink satin ribbon. Not only were they our beloved girls, but they were also breathtakingly beautiful.

Ten-year-old Matthew was his father's best man and was wearing his first tuxedo! He had been scrubbed within an inch of his life that morning, and John had painstakingly combed his blond hair. He was so excited about the occasion that he had put his tuxedo on three times before the wedding. John had to keep saying, "Take it off, Matthew. It's not time yet!" I walked down the aisle on my brother's arm to meet the two identically handsome men, one a smaller version of the other, who were waiting for us at the altar.

We had asked our minister, George K. Jones, to administer communion at the service. We sensed the sacredness of marriage and wanted the sacrament of communion to be part of the sacrament of marriage. At the Lord's table, George blessed our home, our marriage, and our children and asked God to protect and nurture us. After communion and the blessing, John and I and the children sat down on the front row, while all the husbands and wives in the congregation came forward. George blessed their homes, their marriages, and their children.

It was just everything a wedding should be—an affirmation for us of our love and our home, and for the others a reaffirmation of the sanctity of home and the beauty of marriage. In a sense, the whole congregation got married over again. Instead of being anxious or flustered or so excited I couldn't listen, I heard and felt every word of the beautiful ceremony as if it had been spoken in slow motion. I had time to savor each thought and phrase.

After the ceremony, the whole congregation walked down the block and across the street to our home. The house was decked with flowers from lilies to roses to freesias to Queen Anne's lace. Even the front of the house had been painted, and John had given me a surprise gift of five new rose bushes for the bit of garden between the front drive and the sidewalk. Coming from Oregon where roses are so bountiful, I loved his thoughtful present. It was the crowning touch to the dream come true. I would be living with the man I loved in a wonderful old house with happy children and roses beside the front door. The only thing missing was the picket fence!

Topsy Wallace was my helper and the girls' nanny at the time. She preferred keeping house to doing anything else, and since she wasn't married, she loved to keep house for somebody else. One of her talents is cooking; she's an incredible cook. With her own nanny, a black woman who is a fine caterer, Topsy planned and prepared the entire reception. The tables in the dining room were laden with their delicious and beautiful offerings.

We circulated joyfully among our dear friends, rejoicing in their love. Our two sets of relatives visited with one another. My mother, Alice, and John's mother, Caroline, spoke of the hopes and prayers that they each had for our happiness. My mother had faithfully prayed every day that God would send me someone to love me and my two children. Her prayers could not have been answered more lavishly.

The four children, Matthew and Jessica, Juli and Christi, viewed this day as though it were their own wedding day, accepting the congratulations with as much joy as we did. Yet, even in their joy we could see them eyeing one another, trying to determine what the sudden arrival of two more kids would mean to each of them. In a matter of an hour they had each gained a new parent. But in gaining a new parent, and two more siblings, were they losing the parent they had? (That nagging question is one every child of a blended family must face.) Christi and Juli wanted to know if I would still have the same amount of room in my heart for them, now that I had admitted three new people into the place they normally had to themselves. Matt and Jessi had the same concerns about their relationship with John. All four needed the assurance that they would be loved as dearly as before, *and* now by the two of us.

John and I would not be taking a long honeymoon. We had decided just to spend the night in a hotel in downtown Nashville. We would come back to be with the children, who were all staying at my house in Franklin with the grandparents. They needed our presence and our reassurance, we felt, and we wanted to be with them to start the process of blending our two families as soon as possible.

After we had greeted all our friends and enjoyed the food, the laughter, and the delight of the occasion, John and I went upstairs to change our clothes. We had only been in what was now *our* bedroom for five minutes when we heard the first of what seemed like scores of knocks on the door. Four curious voices chimed in with questions: What are you doing in there? When will you be coming out? Do you need anything? Mommy? Do you want me to zip you? Dad, can I come in and change clothes too?

"Patti," said John with a grin, "this is going to be a real experience! Are you sure you're ready for it?"

"Never been more ready," I told him with a hug.

"We're doing fine," we yelled to the kids. "We'll be ready in a minute. Go wait downstairs."

Eight feet scrambled down the uncarpeted stairs, sounding rather like a herd of wild ponies. I guess they were satisfied that the honor of their parents hadn't been compromised. So they turned their attention to white shoe polish and artistic creativity on John's car. The result was a series of congratulatory messages to Mom and Dad across the sides and the windows! No one would be able to miss our new status. This was perhaps the best part of the day for them—next to the cakes!

After I threw the bouquet from the second floor balcony, we ran down the stairs and out to the car through a rain of rose petals and a barrage of good wishes. We hugged and kissed each of the children, drinking in the sight of their little faces filled with hope.

John

The day of our wedding was filled with peace. I was quietly aware that God was in attendance and that

He was pleased. I saw hope on the faces of our children. There was no sense of futility here, only peace.

I was completely in love with Patti. We had attended church with all our families that morning. All day I could not take my eyes from her. Her face was radiant. She looked as though she could not contain her joy. I felt loved.

In the afternoon, Matthew and I went to the church early. We were wearing identically styled tuxedos. I sat down at the piano, and he sat next to me on the bench. A friend who was there took a picture of us as we played a song together. I still cherish that moment. I could see that God had begun the process of healing in Matthew. He had been so hurt by the divorce. The most tender and vivid evidence that I had ever seen of God was the protection that He placed around the hearts of the children. They were so vulnerable to injury, but here they were, joyous. The entire day had a feeling of wholeness about it.

Matthew and I talked as best friends while we waited for the wedding to begin. We played songs and laughed. When the people started coming, we took our places in the small room to the side of the altar. The minister came in and gave us last-minute instructions. Matt checked about every twenty seconds to make sure he had the ring. I was giving Patti the gold ring that my great-grandmother Mamie had worn as her own wedding ring.

Finally it was time. We walked slowly out to our positions at the front of the church. Carol, my sister, began to play the organ music. All eyes watched the back of the church. Jessica came first, followed by Juli, and then Christi, who was her mother's maid of honor. I was overwhelmed with love and joy looking at those three beautiful girls. This wedding was not just for Patti and me, but for the children also.

Then came my bride on the arm of her brother

Ron. Her face was even more radiant than it had been earlier. How beautiful she was! We had already been bonded together in our spirits. We would now become one as man and wife.

The ceremony was quite simple, filled with peace. There was not a dark corner of doubt anywhere in my being. All was light. I knew that this was a blessing from God. After we exchanged our vows and rings, we knelt as the minister prayed for us. Then Patti and I prayed for each other. Finally we took communion. At the Lord's table, we drank fully of Him. Then we moved to the front row of seats as our friends and family members came forward and joined us in the holy sacrament.

As the recessional began, we walked from the altar, followed by our four children. We had been knit together as husband and wife. There was great joy and peace. The past was past. All things were new. God had been merciful.

Patti

My feeling of euphoria was intense as we drove the thirty miles north to Nashville. The feeling of being found, after years of wandering, was so amazing. I can understand why it is worth the search and why people do search so many years for that *right person*. There is a pot of gold at the end of the emotional rainbow, if you can just hang on long enough to get there. I thought my heart would break from the sheer weight of these joyous moments.

I awoke early the next morning with sunlight streaming into our fifth-floor window; the shafts of light were golden around the edges, crisp and crystalline like topaz swords. They fell on John's sleeping face and gilded his hair.

There beside me was my husband. Our first night as man and wife had produced a joy that erased every moment, day, week, and year that we had not shared together. My heart, my body, my hopes, my dreams were forever bonded to him.

O my love, how long and hard I searched for you. How deeply I ached for your love. How I prayed that you existed. I'm content now. I am alive.

My heart is singing a melody of such tenderness and beauty that my lips cannot translate it into sounds for your ears. Please hear it in this moment of shared silence.

How could I have possibly known that in a few short months I would come to regard this man as my most dangerous enemy!

PART II

"Cleanse thou me from secret faults"
Psalm 19:12

O God who made fire,
O God who made ice,
Have mercy upon us
As amid both we walk.

P.T.

9

Becoming a Family

Patti

The plastic holly wreath greeted us from the back gate as we drove into our enclosed back yard from the alley. Though it was August, just two months after our wedding, the wreath still hung where we had put it not long after our one-night honeymoon. Each time we came home it greeted us with its dusty leaves and wilted bow.

I've noticed how lovers often tend to view certain objects as symbols of beauty, private declarations of love, encoded statements about their hearts' feelings toward each other. The symbols don't need any intrinsic value or beauty. We had several such symbols, and the Christmas wreath was one of them.

Before it came to hang on our back fence, it rested among tennis racquets, Nikes, and gym bags in the trunk of John's car. Before that, Matt and Jessi would tie it to the front bumper of the car just before they started out with John for the twelve-hour drive home to Grandma and Grandpa Thompsons' for Christmas.

So the wreath represented family. It represented home. It represented hope for things to come. And here on our fence in the middle of summer, it represented the celebration of sharing love—a sort of forever Christmas.

But in spite of the warm sentiment, it was

ugly—bedraggled, faded, gray, covered with dust and grime from miles of highway driving. I kept thinking that we should take it down, but sentiment always seemed to win out. More than once our neighbor remarked that it was certainly an oddity and definitely ugly. She is a dear friend who could single-handedly uphold the genteel propriety of the South, and would probably have found even a real holly wreath gauche in the middle of summer; a plastic one certainly gave scandalous new dimensions to the word *tacky*. Several weeks later, it mysteriously disappeared, saggy bow and all. I suspect it succumbed to her unflagging sense of decorum!

Looking back now, I can see that the bow was an apt picture of our marriage. We were still overflowing with love for each other, but occasionally we would notice that perhaps the bows of love weren't as bright and new as the first euphoria of our love had painted them. Even the children's excitement and joy was fading a bit.

This afternoon John and I were returning home from the grocery store. The children had reluctantly agreed to stay home while John and I went shopping. Having someone to share these mundane tasks with made them so enjoyable that trips to the Kroger supermarket had become romantic outings!

John and I had lived each day of the past two months as if it were a banquet. John's time schedule was his own to regulate, so there were many days that we spent entirely and happily together. Our joy was marred only by the fact that, due to a custody arrangement, Matthew and Jessica could spend only every other weekend with us, though sometimes during the week we'd get to share a supper with them. But our time with them was just too brief; John would begin to get a faraway look in his eyes when he hadn't seen Matt and Jessi for a few days.

Although the love we were sharing and the home we were creating seemed to bring John joy, there were still obvious moments when grief would surface. Our love wasn't mending this one area of sorrow in his life. I believed that love must eventually heal all types of bruising and brokenness, so it was a frustration for me to see him occasionally sink into depression over the children's absence from our house.

But this was a happy weekend. On Friday after school we had picked Matt and Jessi up at their mother's house in Nashville. We had gone out to eat, as we usually did, and then taken everyone to a movie. We had spent Saturday cleaning, playing, and grocery shopping. It had been a usual weekend, so far.

John and I began unloading the many bags of food it takes to keep a family of this size going, and he called for the children to come help us carry them into the kitchen.

The response was slow. First Juli came dragging from the far corner of the yard. Her tanned face was streaked with tears, and her lip was quivering. From the opposite far corner Matthew walked reluctantly. He, too, had been crying. When we asked what had happened, no one wanted to talk. Jessi and Christi were pale and wide-eyed and declared, "We don't know anything."

I took Juli to our bedroom while John and Matt headed for the library. At five o'clock, John called a family meeting in the library. On the sofa in front of us sat our four children, their faces apprehensive as to what this first official family pow-wow might bring. Matt and Juli were still sniffling.

John

Christi and Jessica sat on the two ends of the floral couch. They didn't know too much of what the uproar was about. They just knew that the tone of the meeting was serious, so they were the first ones to answer this hurriedly called conference. They each rested an elbow on the couch's arms and stared off into a distant point on the ceiling.

Patti came in next and sat on one of the small chairs across from the couch. I waited, standing, as Juli and Matt entered with their heads down. They reluctantly took the middle seats on the couch next to each other. I had already talked with Matthew, and Patti had talked with Juli, so we knew the heart of this first major confrontation.

I asked Matt to tell us what all this was about. He started to talk, but suddenly stopped and put his head down. He was crying again. That started Juli weeping, while Jessi and Chris stared deeper into the ceiling.

As I looked at the four of them, I remembered the day two months before when they had stood on the front staircase for pictures after our wedding. We were married on Father's Day, and I was doubly proud of these four. They had looked and acted so beautiful on that joyous occasion filled with hope. Now I hurt for them.

Between sobs, the story came out. Matthew was terribly hurt at having to leave here after being with his daddy for just two days. And not only that, but the two girls he had loved calling "sister" at the wedding got to stay behind with someone who wasn't really their daddy. That afternoon the hurt got so bad he told Juli exactly how he felt in terms that weren't complimentary to her. I wasn't her dad—I was his. She had no claim on me, or so he felt. The result was a shouting match.

The issue underneath was that they both wanted

as much love as they could get. They had become used to being jostled about during their parents' divorces. This new union was a thing of hope for them; yet, they had many fears and anxieties.

That night we talked together about how God was giving us new rooms in our hearts. We weren't crowding anyone out, but were expanding the places in which we held love. Then all six of us prayed together. When we finished, Matt and Juli hugged each other. Christi and Jessi were quiet, but I knew they understood more than they let on. And they got in on the hugging afterwards.

God began a healing in us all that night. We had had a small breakthrough toward intimacy. We would need many more.

Later that night while Patti was asleep and I held her close to the curve of my body, I thought long and hard about what it meant to be a father to all four of these children.

I am a father. I am a step-father.

The distinction between these two roles has become less and less defined for me as I grow older and, I hope, better at being both.

When Patti and I married, I was determined to be the best father and step-father that I could be. Paradoxically, when the mother of my children had remarried, I, like most parents, was somewhat fearful of *my* children's living most of the time with a step-parent in their lives. My childhood hadn't prepared me for this at all. My home was a stable one, and I never even had to imagine my life without my parents together. So this was new territory for me.

Of the many weaknesses I have, being a poor father is not one of them. I love Matthew and Jessica completely and would do anything for them. After the divorce, I was thrown into the position of being a father from a distance most of the time. I had to try to fit two weeks of living into every other weekend. I fell into the same traps I'm sure many newly divorced fathers fall into.

At first I tried to fill the times together with as many activities as there were hours in a Saturday. On Friday nights, we were euphoric at the prospect of just being together. We savored the hours as a vacation from the pain of separation. The house I had purchased included bedrooms for each of the children, and together we decorated them with great care. I wanted the children to have a sense of home, even on weekends. But their rooms would stay amazingly clean, because we ended up sleeping in the same king-sized bed, not willing to spend any time apart that wasn't absolutely necessary. Sometimes when they were asleep I would lie awake just watching them, storing in my memory pictures of how they looked asleep, unguarded, vulnerable, natural.

Our Saturdays were filled with trips to museums and parks. We would go to movies and almost always ate out. But after a few months of this frenetic activity, we made a joint decision: We just wanted to be together, and constant effort to make up for lost time wasn't necessary. So we began just staying home and spending time together. Those turned out to be the best times. Doing nothing was everything!

On Sunday mornings the sadness always set in. We tried not to think ahead to the afternoon when we would have to separate again. We would go to church, then to lunch, but always we counted the hours until I took them back to their mother.

At lunch on Sundays I could always spot the broken families. They were the fathers and children who seemed to cling to one another. The sight made me angry, angry at a society that seemingly overlooked this cost of divorce and had come to accept broken homes as just one of many hazards indigenous to the fast pace at which we live. And angry at myself for having become a statistic.

When Patti and I had begun to date, and to include the children in our activities, there was a noticeable excitement among them. Jessica stopped asking me, as she had almost every Sunday afternoon since she was very small, if I was happy. She knew that I was! The anticipation of a new life together was on the children's faces.

Now, after the marriage, the realities had set in.

I was in a completely new role to Juli and Christi. For Matthew and Jessica, I was no longer just their dad, but two other people's step-dad.

What is a step-father? I learned quickly that the word *step* in this usage is sadly in error. We tend to think of a step-parent as someone removed by a "step" from the real relationship. True, a blood parent is still a blood parent, regardless of a divorce court decree, but a step-parent is not just a partner for one of the real parents. In our situation I am, in actual time spent, a step-father for over ten months of the year to Christi and Juli. Matthew and Jessica also have a step-father for nearly the same amount of time. I spend more time with my step-children than I do with my blood children. We have to face these real-life situations.

This is not to say that step-parents take the place of blood parents. But the needs of the children are not met solely by a monthly child support check. The word *step* means the act of putting one foot in front of the other and the distance covered by doing so. This literal definition is much closer to the truth than the meaning of "removal" that is so common. It is, in fact, a very real picture of the step-parent.

I have grown to love Juli and Christi very much. Every morning at 7:15 we drive to school together and often talk about Matthew and Jessica and the chronicles of our literally extended family, extended not only by marriage but also by miles. These are the real-life times, like comforting and hugging Christi when she didn't make the cheerleading squad one year. Or waiting an extra hour in the car after school for the next year's squad to be posted so she could see whether she made it. (She did!) It is going for a ride with Juli after she returns from a visit with her father, and listening to her cry at having to leave and come home to Nashville. I tell her I know how it feels, and I cry, missing Matt and Jessi. Then, in the midst of tears we laugh, as I tell Juli that it looks like we're stuck with each other.

These are the "steps" we take together. A step is a very short distance, and it takes many of them to get anywhere. Somewhere in there is a definition of a step-parent I can live with.

Patti

Sometimes the process of blending our two families was like ice cubes in a high speed blender—a lot of noise and flying chips. Christi, Juli, and I had lived a rather quiet, orderly existence. We had had our share of dirty socks and wet towels, but the addition of three more people with their dirty socks and wet towels made the laundry room look like a war zone, and not all of it got to the laundry room. We not only had three additional people in the house that summer, but two of them were males.

We heard many "Oooh, yuk" comments coming from our three prissy girls. While Jessica may have been undisturbed by the habits of her brother before our marriage, now she had two older sisters, and her tastes and perceptions changed accordingly.

I became so frustrated with the state of Matthew's bedroom that I stopped going into it. I would send John in, and even with his masculine tolerance he would emerge a little green around the gills.

Finally I confronted Matthew.

"I'm sick of the mess you are making of your room. In fact, everywhere you go, you leave a trail of crud behind you. Furthermore, I am sick of having to yell at you. You are making me feel like the wicked old step-mother. I hate yelling at you."

"That's OK, Patti," he said with a boyish warmth and concern in his voice. "My mom has to yell at me all the time, too."

Well, duly disarmed, I threw up my hands and gave up for the day. I couldn't win over such a flawless response!

Having a teenaged son has been something of an adjustment for me. He is a bamboozling mixture of woman-killer charm and little boy naughtiness, and he knows how special he is to John and can use that knowledge to manipulate relationships. It was hard for me to get to know him because of that, and also because I wanted him to like me.

One day I called Matt in to have a showdown. I told him my frustrations, that I thought he was emotionally and mentally doublecrossing me. He was only eleven, but he understood perfectly! I told him that I thought he was setting me up so that he could work his dad against me, and how angry that made me. I wanted to love him, I said, but those things hurt, and then I'd feel guilty because I wanted to cream him!

He sat there as if he were eighty years old, shaking his head as though to say, "I understand, I understand." Then he broke down and cried, and I could see his sweet vulnerability, and of course he was no longer the enemy.

"Patti, I do understand," he finally said. "I'll try to be better."

Then I began to cry. "Oh, Matthew, I am so sorry, but I have felt such meanness toward you."

"It's all right, Patti, I understand."

The result was a wonderful openness between us, our first real appointment with honesty. We told each other what we were afraid of, what hurt our feelings, what made us angry.

At the end of our conversation, Matthew went out to talk to John. John asked him how the interview had gone. Matthew shrugged his shoulders and said, "Dad, she just had a lot to get off her chest. I just had to sit there and listen to her. She's better now. Don't worry."

That was another breakthrough. There is no blending in a family without honesty between every member of the family. You can't pussyfoot around or walk on eggshells with any member. Love is aggressive. When there's a fissure, something broken underneath the surface, there's no sense covering it up. You might as well go for the truth and get it out, especially with kids. It's amazing how much they can deal with forthrightly if you do.

There were other run-ins among the children that summer, a sense of rivalry, as well as of exploration, learning to know one another's strengths and weaknesses. But along with that was an underlying sense of love and unity. And a lot of laughs. The laughs got us over the awkwardness of being new to one another and were as important in the process of becoming a family as the times we wept together.

Matthew is good at creating laughs, sometimes in the least appropriate places—as for instance, in church. We were all in church one Sunday, with the four children and their cousin Christopher filling the pew beside John and me. For a while there was the normal fidgeting and sniffling and looking for cough drops. (Have you ever noticed how raw children's throats get during a sermon?). But then I noticed that Juli was making notes, presumably not on the sermon, and beside her Matt was drawing something, with Christopher excitedly waiting for the finished product.

As we began the communion service I felt a slight tremor rocking the pew. When I looked up, the children were all holding their mouths, but not quite suppressing their giggles. Except for Matthew, whose angelic face was tilted up with the light from the stained-glass window highlighting his blond hair and rosy cheeks—and his look of holy mischief. Whatever was in his hand had the undivided attention of four decidedly irreverent children. Being known as the "pew sheriff" who, according to the children, would probably pinch the apostles if they happened to talk in church, I grabbed Matthew's clenched hand and extracted a drawing of a small boy wearing blue jeans, drawn from the rear point of view with a hole torn in the paper, *right at the little boy's seat,* which, when placed over a clenched fist with the hole centered on the crease in one's fist . . . well, you get the picture!

At such times, John is no help, because he is as much of a kid as the children. They all looked to him as if to say, "Dad, control Mom. She's getting out of hand." John patted my leg with that honey-darling-sugar-lamb-calm-down-and-return-to-your-praying look. It's obvious where Matthew gets his charm!

For our first Thanksgiving, we decided to take the whole family to John's home in Pennsylvania. It would be our first family trip, and we were all excited and expectant. The children were packed days in advance. Matt and Jessi were anxious to show Christi and Juli where their Grandma and Grandpa lived and how neat the house was.

When we began to pack the station wagon, we almost gave up. Neither John nor I realized how large a family we had. There were six people, plus pillows, books, clothes, dolls, toy guns, Matt's FBI kit (that was the year he was into spying and was known as Agent Thompson), a coffee Thermos, baskets of munchies, wet wipes—masses of survival equipment for this twelve-hour trip.

The poor children looked like happy Vienna sausages stuffed into a can. We had to stop every thirty minutes, or so it seemed, to let them rotate. Two were in the very back, stretched out over suitcases softened by blankets and pillows. The other two were in the back seat. Nobody was really happy with the rotation. Invariably when one wanted to sleep it was not time to be on the pallet. And when one wanted to read it wasn't time to be in the back seat.

At one point, John and I began to notice a not too faint, toxic odor.

"Juli did it!"

"No, I didn't! Jessica did it."

"No I didn't! I didn't! Daddy, make them stop saying I tooted. Besides, Christi did it!"

"No, I didn't. Matt did it!"

In his very best impersonation of Ed Sullivan, Matt said, "Ladies and gentlemen, that was Mr. Billy Joel. Let's give him a hand!"

For six hundred miles something was dying in the back seat, and nobody ever did it! But every time Matt would say, "that was Mr. Billy Joel," we'd have to laugh. In fact, we laughed so hard that for a while there was general pandemonium.

That trip provided one other inside family joke, summed up in the line, "Hey, Juli, show us your legs."

Juli had just been rotated from the pallet in the back of the car to the back seat. In an effort to stretch out her eleven-year-old frame, she stuck her leg through the space between the front seats created by the arm rest's being down. There, not ten inches from my eyes, was a leg so shiny, so slick and smooth, it could have reflected the rays of the sun.

"Juli," I said. "When did you start shaving your legs?"

Silence. The first total silence I had heard in months.

"When, Juli?"

'Uh, oh, umm, let's see. When did I shave my legs?"

"That's the question, Juli."

"Uh, well, er." Snickers punctuated the heavy air as Juli looked for a trap door on the floor of the car. "Mom, I meant to ask, I was going to ask. It was an accident. I mean, the hairs were just so long. . . . I was going to tell you, but I guess I forgot."

Finally, in a whisper, she said, "I dunno, Mom. It just happened."

I suppressed my amusement. After all, it wasn't as though I had missed her baptism. But mothers do like to be informed about such things and have some room for input. "Just try not to rush your leap into womanhood," I sighed.

That trip was a good microcosm of the forced blending process. In such a small space barriers come down, kids feel comfortable with one another, and there are bad smells as well as funny jokes. But accepting the bad smells and laughing at the jokes are both necessary parts of the process.

10

Giving Up Illusions

Patti

he phone was ringing as I walked into the house from the back yard. Before I answered it, I breathed a prayer that God would not only help me keep my wits about me, but also enable me to actually say something of importance. This would be the second radio interview I'd done today from the sunroom of our home. Technology has advanced communications to the point that by phone one can take part in a "live" radio interview being broadcast thousands of miles away.

This particular broadcast was coming from Oklahoma. Of all the states I'd just as soon forget, this surely did top my list. I picked up the phone, and the voice at the other end asked for Patti Roberts. As I started to explain that I was now Patti Thompson, John, who had been reading at the other end of the room, got up and walked out.

The week prior to our June wedding, my book *Ashes to Gold* came off the presses. The timing couldn't have been more awkward for me. To have a book released about the failure of my last marriage while I was taking the first steps down the aisle toward

The wedding party. (Clockwise: John, Christi, Jessica, Juli, Matthew, and me.)

Off to the honeymoon. The children announced to the world just where we'd be!

(Left to right from rear: Christi, Matthew, John,
Juli [holding Miss Kitty], Jessica, and me.
Pepper sits reluctantly.)

Photo by E. W. Reames.

John at work on El Shaddai.

Doing vocals for Hope of the Heart album at the
Scruggs Studio, Nashville.

Working at my desk in the sun room, trying to catch up on correspondence generated by <u>Ashes to Gold</u>. The response of readers was overwhelming.

Granny Holcombe and what is left of one of her heavenly pies.

Baby John with his precious Mamie.

Here we are on July 4 at Sweet Springs Farm, home of our dear friends Peter and Barbara Jenkins.

John and I at our Thanksgiving table in 1985. I was expecting, and we had SO much to be thankful for that year.

Matthew and Jessica in Alaska.

John and I with Canon. Baby's first photo session!

Photo by Hank Widick.

building my new life with John was classic bad timing. But it couldn't be helped.

I had written *Ashes to Gold,* sent it in to my publisher, and had the galleys in my hand before I ever met John Thompson. But our meeting, courtship, and marriage happened so quickly that I had to do the promotional work for the book during the first months of our marriage.

There were phone, magazine, and newspaper interviews and a hectic national book tour in which I went from city to city, at each stop being subjected to the inevitable questions regarding my divorce from Richard Roberts and the working of the Oral Roberts organization. The press, it seemed, were only slightly interested in the story of what I had learned about life and marriage; they were keenly curious about the persons of Oral and Richard Roberts. More than once I'd ended up defending them to the press. The writers seemed to have a pent-up store of anger waiting to be poured out on the Robertses, and more than once they had used my story to vent their own hatred. I was often caught in the cross-fire between my own feelings and those of the press.

In addition, there was the staggering fact that I daily talked about the demise and death of one marriage while I tried to open myself to the building of another. It was a classic example of the fact that while the blood of Christ covers even the sin of divorce, we are yet left living with the fruits of what we have sown. The sufficiency of the atonement and the immutability of God's law of sowing and reaping coexist. All this added up to a very odd time for me—taxing and embarrassing. But it was John who was suffering most.

He viewed our love as if it were as delicate and untainted as a newly blossomed camellia. The fact that we were now having to deal publicly with my past life was, to him, like a hairy brute crushing the camellia in his dirty hand, discoloring, bruising and marring it.

For John it was a breach of good taste to have to deal with the years that I was Patti Roberts. It was bad timing. It was regrettable.

I could understand his irritability about the situation. But the release of the book and the subsequent promotional tour were already contracted for before our meeting. Even though it was awkward, it was a fact that couldn't be changed.

So day after day John heard of the inner workings of the Oral Roberts Evangelistic Association, the public face of marital bliss, and the private torment beneath the surface of Richard and Patti watching their crippled union die a hideous death. Day after day John became less tolerant of my past. It wasn't the joy and celebration of John and Patti's union that was on everybody's lips, but the failure of love in Richard and Patti's lives.

More and more John began to shut out my past. He would get up and walk out of the room if anything prior to April 13, 1983, was mentioned. It was as if he had become so overdosed on the saga of Patti Roberts that he shut out all of my past and lived in denial that she ever existed. Suddenly I felt as if any part of me prior to April 13, 1983, wasn't permitted to live. I could sympathize with his reasoning, but I was left hanging in limbo with no reference points—no memories, no identity, and no past—as though I had arrived on the planet at age thirty-five, delivered in a golden egg with no return address. I had simply appeared out of some foggy cloud and dropped into John's life.

That attitude also denied me any sharing of grief. As a result, I felt thoroughly isolated and very much unhealed. I resented John for loving only the present and future me. I needed him to embrace the past me just as urgently as he needed me to forget her. It wasn't that I wanted to lolligag around in the past, but it was necessary to deal with what had just been published.

The promotional events related to the book were not really a surprise to John. Prior to our marriage we had discussed the book and the impact of its publication in our lives. John had seemed so broad-shouldered and unflappable about it all that I had marveled at his strength. In fact, he had been a refuge for me, a place to find comfort and cover from the rigors that arise from a controversial book. But that was before publication. Conjecture and theory proved inaccurate when we were faced with actuality.

I wrote *Ashes to Gold* in the hope that others who had suffered in broken relationships might find the same road of hope I was in the process of finding. But now the book seemed a destructive force.

I hadn't counted on the fact that, though John was talking big, brave, and strong, inside of him was a tremulous little boy who was saying, "Hey, what about me?" And at the same time a full-blown male ego was booming out, "Hey, what about me?" Any male with a well-formed ego would probably have chafed under the circumstances. John was not only temporarily obscured by his wife, but worse yet, also by his wife's ex-husband. Our camellias were definitely being bruised.

The mail I received on the book was of two kinds. Daily I had letters which said, "Thank you, I feel as if you've written my own story." But I also got negative letters. Some readers felt I had spoken out of turn about differences I had had with Oral Roberts. Most were more upset abut the theological differences we had than they were about the dissolution of the family.

Then there were readers who sent treatises and sermons and quoted Scripture on divorce and remarriage. I read all of these, as I did all my mail. One letter in particular, with an accompanying booklet, told me that if I really loved God I would remarry Richard—never mind that he had been married to his second wife for four years and that I had just remarried. The man quoted so much Scripture that I held his letter and wept deep sobs of regret and confusion.

The very idea that I could have missed God's leading so completely gave me the emptiest feeling of futility. I knew I had felt God's peace when I married John. Had I felt a lie? I had believed myself to be free to marry John, since our former spouses had already remarried. Had I misunderstood the law? Was I indeed living outside of God's will? Must I now leave John and try to convince Richard Roberts to remarry me?

John sat me down after I showed him that letter. "Patti," he said. "You've got to choose either the law or grace. You have got to choose the righteousness of Christ, or you have to provide your own righteousness.

"As far as a scriptural basis for remarriage, there are as many interpretations as there are biblical scholars. I don't feel comfortable debating on grounds of Scripture the issue of whether we should have gotten married. If we do that, then we are offering our rationale to anybody else who decides on remarriage. We can't do that. We had to seek God on whether we should marry. We found His peace, and we experienced His blessings. God has joined us together and given us a basis for a true marriage. The interpretation of Scripture can be debated. God's grace and mercy cannot."

John's wisdom was very comforting to me. Not only did it help me deal with the criticism arising from the book, but it also reaffirmed my love for John. There were times in those first months of our marriage when great waves of love and adoration for John welled up in me. I once caught myself beginning to form the words "I worship you" to him. In a profound way I had made him my idol, the object of my intense desire. I guess it wasn't surprising that my devotion for John even eclipsed my devotion to God.

My desire to absorb and be absorbed, to be totally enveloped in this loving experience, was evidence that I had chosen the gift that God had given me even over the Giver. If God's mercy was to prevail, John inevitably had to topple off the throne he wrongly occupied in my heart. Gradually the throne began to sway a bit, then shimmy, and soon it was to heave and lunge and with a great crash dislodge my idol.

Eventually, when the mail came each day, John and I both breathed sighs of relief when it contained only letters and not stacks of bills. The combining of our two households had proven to be a very costly venture. I had entered our marriage with a fat mortgage payment, a car payment, clothing store bills, and an assortment of credit card charges. John had a mortgage payment and other bills, so we planned to sell his house. At the outset, I wasn't too worried about our financial concerns because John didn't seem to be worried. I'd told him about my financial obligations and that, contrary to popular belief, I was solidly middle class rather than wealthy. That didn't matter to him. He said we'd make it. I took comfort in his confidence.

John and I agreed that he would take over all our financial business. He was to pay the bills, budget the money, and bear the weight of our debt. After so many years of going it alone, that was a tremendous relief to me—a wonderful gift. There had been many months that I'd struggled to make ends meet. Now I could sit back and just be the wife, mother, homemaker—the ultimate luxury for a woman who had lived nearly six years as a single parent.

But all too soon after the wedding, the mail began to bring us an assortment of unwelcome letters. The bank sent overdraft notices. The creditors sent friendly reminders, and the phone began ringing with bill collectors. Not wanting to question my new husband's financial management skills, I fretted privately instead of confronting the issue directly.

Occasionally I'd find a stack of unopened bills postmarked one or two or even three months earlier. The intimation of impending doom began to trickle into my thoughts. I also noticed that when John wrote a check he would often fail to enter it into the register. Alarm bells rang.

Was I to chalk this up to the eccentricities of his 170 IQ? Or was I to admit that my husband was intentionally pitching us headlong into bankruptcy? He became short-tempered with me when I finally did ask questions. Admittedly by this time my questions sounded more like accusations than questions. (The throne was definitely shimmying now!)

My family were law-abiding, bill-paying folks. During all my growing up days I saw money handled in a very precise way. First God got His 10 percent tithe, then Uncle Sam got his percentage, then the rest went to pay bills. By the tenth day of each month, my mom and dad had mailed out all of their bills. Whatever money happened to be left over went for food, clothing, savings accounts, and a little put away for vacations. If there wasn't much left over, well, that was reflected in our reduced standard of living—and no vacations.

These financial habits had been passed down to both my parents from their parents, and their grandparents before that. Even though I had long ago adopted the fine American tradition of debt, still at the very core of me were the same attitudes toward owing that my parents, grandparents, and great-grandparents had shared. I knew that John's parents held the same attitudes about their financial dealings as did my parents. Underneath it all, John himself held to these same values; it was just that somewhere along the way the values had been sacrificed to the god of expediency. I feared not knowing the whole truth about our finances. In my mind I constructed a scenario of total financial collapse.

Finally I had to know. I pleaded with John to sit down with me and explain exactly what our financial situation was, to describe what was threatening the family's security and our trust in each other.

Painfully, John began to unburden a hidden history of long overdue debts and countless other obligations.

The throne had toppled.

My fears of financial failure had come true.

The dam of trust in my husband I had thought would protect me gave way and unleashed a torrent of anger, hurt, and fear.

It is ironic that before our marriage I valued John for his honesty and transparency. He had told me much about his past life that could have been damaging, but he had trusted me with it. I had valued that in him so much that it never occurred to me there was also in John a great fear—fear of disclosure and of letting me know something that might really upset me.

There were further complications. When we married, John and I agreed that he would look out for my career and ministry. Whatever I did in the way of pursuing my singing, he would attend to. He was to be responsible for my transition from a solo career to one that would join our two talents. This seemed to square with my understanding of biblical teaching on the roles we each were to accept. Perhaps if I had been a nurse and he a fireman it wouldn't have been appropriate for him to manage my affairs. But we were both in the same field, had similar callings, and wished to work together. So in this case it was entirely appropriate.

The hitch in our plan was that to the public I was known as Patti Roberts rather than Patti Thompson.

Both of us felt that because I was no longer a Roberts, we should retire the professional use of the name. Now it appeared that in retiring the name, John was retiring me, too. Opportunities for singing seemed to have slid right by us, and he made little effort to involve us in any public ministry. Looking back now, I sincerely believe that John was following God's plan, but at the time it looked like passive and neglectful behavior. It seemed as if my work was of little value to him. And I couldn't see that sitting in this house for a year or five years, or maybe the rest of my life, could fit in with the calling I felt on my life.

Not only was John not providing me with any ticket back into the community in which I felt called to minister, but he also seemed to be taking away every credential I thought I had. "Patti Roberts" was fading away. Yet, "Patti Thompson" was not emerging.

When God begins a restoration process, many, and sometimes all, aspects of one's former identity seem to die as God forms a new identity. But that death, like any other, causes pain. "He must increase, but I must decrease" (John 3:30 RSV) was a noble aspiration for me. I did want God to be preeminent in my life. But when I saw my identity decrease to nothing, I was angry and hurt. Even more, I was furious. What I had really wanted was for Jesus to increase only as long as it didn't cost my sense of self.

But I couldn't be furious with Jesus. So for now I heaped the blame on John for what looked like the end of my idyllic love and my dreams, not to mention my career.

I began to wake up in the mornings with a feeling of sadness. By noon, my sadness became anger. By suppertime, anger became despair. The weight of the financial problems and the career confusion was taking its toll. I was buckling beneath it all—angry at being denied the full truth concerning our finances, but fearful of the unknown. When I added up all the problems, I believed they meant that I was not loved. This was the most devastating feeling of all. I was alone. Stranded.

11

What Do You Do with Brokenness?

John

T he statistics don't need to be quoted; we are bombarded by the facts. Brokenness has become epidemic. Yet we seem to treat it as some mass inconvenience, simply a by-product of the feverish search for gratification. We cannot stand in a grocery check-out line, watch the morning news, walk through an airport, or attend a family reunion without being aware of brokenness of some kind.

Our children sit in classrooms in which an average of half their classmates come from broken homes. Ministers, mechanics, doctors, teachers, aerobic instructors, Christians, Jews—all have a legion among their ranks who have been devastated by divorce.

The great panacea for this epidemic is movement, motion. If your life isn't working out in a certain job, find another. If your marriage is in trouble, end it; there is a better relationship to be found. If your friends aren't always friends, forget them; there are others.

All of the emotion I had created in my own life produced nothing. I had not found peace. One night it came to a halt. It was not a noisy, screeching halt, but a gradual and quiet numbing. I was at the end of myself.

About three months before I met Patti, I was unable to sleep one night and got up to play the piano. I usually had tremendous patience with myself, but this night I was not even on my own side. In my mind I reviewed the past decade: two failed marriages, some good music, my precious Matthew and Jessica removed from my everyday life—and a very irresponsible attitude toward my business dealings. I felt the guilt of failure in many areas. That night the piano offered no comfort.

Unable to soothe my feelings with writing, as I usually did, I got in the car and drove aimlessly. I ended up at Anchor High Marina, where I had once docked a boat I used to own. After my first divorce, I actually lived on it for a year. It was a thirty-six-foot sportsfisherman that could sleep up to six people.

I love the water. Nashville is bordered on the north and east by two medium-sized lakes created by dams across the Cumberland and Stones rivers. Old Hickory Lake, on the north, was where I had docked the boat. I got out of the car and walked out into the docks where my old slip was, an end slip that looked directly out on the lake. Across the cove I could see the lights from the lock where boats could be lowered the ninety feet down from the lake to the Cumberland River. This night the water was very calm and the lake looked like glass.

My eyes saw a beautiful, serene sight. What my heart felt was the opposite of serene. I had no calm in me. In the quiet of that moment, I reached out to God. I loved Him, but I had not been close to Him for a long time. Basically I had run my own life, occasionally asking Him to "post-bless" my decisions. I would do as I pleased and then turn to God to get me out of one bad situation after another.

There on the dock I was like a soldier in a foxhole, facing the enemies of my own pride and stubborn will. I felt as though I were in danger of losing everything.

Finally, in the midst of this battle, I was able for the very first time in my life to give God all of me. The chorus of the song I wrote that night expressed my heart:

> Lord, prepare me
> To be a sanctuary,
> Pure and holy,
> Tried and true,
> And with thanksgiving
> I'll be a living
> Sanctuary for you.*

I later finished the song "Sanctuary" with my partner, Randy Scruggs, and we recorded it on an album by our friend Jessi Dixon. The force of those words was a turning point in my life. I meant business with God that night. I was willing to do it His way, whatever that might end up costing. I walked away from the dock a person who had begun the process of dying to self that is at the heart of Christ's teaching.

Nothing changed immediately. But God began to set in motion a series of painful and joyous changes that would bring me closer than ever before to what I knew was His will for my life. I began to experience a deepening peace within myself. I had been over-burdened with my weakness and failures, but I was aware that God would help me face them head on. I was beginning a long, difficult journey. The enemies of pride and will that I had been able to identify and admit were formidable foes. But my commitment to follow God was sure. I began the journey with repentance and restitution.

God's mercy is a very real thing to me. As I became able to face myself, I could see God more clearly. I was not a murderer or a drug dealer, but I had emotional closets that were full of hidden things. I knew where I needed to start.

When my first marriage began to fall apart, I grew disillusioned and bitter. My view of myself was not good, and I withdrew into an attitude of apathy and unconcern. I have fought the problem of procrastination all my life, but this was different. I just didn't care any more.

In the three years before the divorce I produced a number of successful contemporary Christian albums. But after the divorce, I canceled the ones I was scheduled to work on and basically walked away from the whole business. I was living with such guilt because of my failed marriage that I felt staying in the Christian music industry put me into a hypocritical life I could not live. For the next years I lived in a state of confusion. *I* chose what to call totally wrong. *I* chose what to rationalize as a weakness of someone with "an artistic temperament." So for the next six years I continued to neglect many of my financial obligations. I was being "artistic."

If I were going to be true to what I had promised God, I knew this was the first issue that needed dealing with. Before Patti and I married, I called the institution to which I owed the largest amount of money and made arrangements to begin paying not only the original debt but also the large amount of interest levied against me. However, I still battled with my pride. I couldn't tell anyone who knew me how I'd procrastinated and sloughed off this responsibility.

When Patti and I began dating, I told her there were some money problems that needed clearing up. But I was never able to tell her how lax I had been. I had built enough equity in the music company I owned to cover my delinquent obligations, and if I had to, I would sell the company. But I really preferred to handle my financial problem privately. I didn't want to reveal this weakness to Patti. My pride would not allow me to be completely honest. And so I hurt the person I loved most. If I had been honest from the first and communicated the full extent of the problem and my intent to correct it, she would have understood. But I never gave her the chance.

Now, with the anger and the threat of annulment in the air, I went back through seven years of bills, documents, and receipts. I made dozens of phone calls and sent as many letters. I was determined to get my "closets" cleaned out, and this debt was the first of those hidden things. More came tumbling out when I opened the door. There were people of whom I needed to ask forgiveness. There were those to whom I needed to offer restitution. Some accepted, some forgave, and some did both.

But in spite of the fact that I was struggling to rectify our financial problems and straighten things out, Patti was still angry and hurt. She seemed to have collapsed on the inside.

The issues we were dealing with in our marriage and in our family are the issues of life. God wants our wholeness. He is never content to stop with mere surface problems. It is true that I had hurt Patti through my negligence. Solving the money problems was a specific job that I had to face. But it was just a starting place. God intended for the healing to be far more in depth than our becoming financially solvent. God desired to heal the bruises and wounds that were so deeply imbedded in us we hardly knew they were there. He was going for the roots of my procrastination and my fear of facing failure. And He seemed to be going for some of Patti's roots as well.

12

Is There Any Hope?

Patti

A friend suggested that I needed some counseling. Perhaps it would help to have an unbiased third party with whom I could discuss not only John's actions, but also my reactions. Right here in Franklin I found a psychiatric social worker, who happened also to be a Christian. I felt safe with her and began to see her twice a week.

Hour after hour I poured out my feelings of despair, only to find that at the bottom of my despair was yet another cistern filled to the brim with the accumulation of years of rage. Even though they felt lethal, my experiences with John were merely a thin layer on top of many other feelings of helplessness, abandonment, and anger.

But when friends suggested that perhaps I had suffered long enough and should consider divorce, or possibly annulment on the grounds of deception, I balked. Yes, I was throwing "annulment" at John, but down deep I couldn't face the end of this marriage with any more peace than I could face the continuation of it.

I would look at John—so beautiful, so gifted not only with brains but also with astounding musical ability, so sensitive, so loving, but, sadly, so damaged —and I would be so frustrated I could almost scream. What on earth had caused a man filled with such remarkable potential for success to so willingly sabotage the very hope of it at nearly every level? What had struck down the normal feelings of responsibility?

A shadowy thought began to trail me. Was this happening because I wasn't worth an explanation? Did my personhood not merit the sharing of this obligation before our marriage? Why hadn't he loved me enough to tell me the truth before we were married? Why hadn't he loved himself enough? With every look at him my eyes screamed, "How dare you? How could you?" If he had feelings of self-loathing, I did my best to increase them.

For the first time in my life, I felt the desire to kill. How very strange—because I wanted to kill the very one I had loved more deeply, more passionately, and with more abandonment than I had ever loved anyone. It wasn't just because my husband appeared to be a financial failure and hadn't told me. I hated him most because the man to whom I had given everything I was and hoped to become appeared to have said, "So what?"

I had yet to understand something absolutely essential regarding the nature of a God-given marriage: Love, when it is real, will cause all that is unlike itself to bubble to the surface. All that is unlovely and unloving will become evident when the light of real love enters a relationship. Love cannot coexist with a less noble force. To be true to itself, love must consume all that is unlike it. That produces conflict, disclosure, heat, and flames.

But, love consumes its antithesis with *love* rather than with condemnation, blame, or force.

John's procrastination and fear of confrontation, as well as my harsh judgments regarding his failures, were only a few of the many "less noble" things that were going to surface.

Unfortunately, John and I weren't the only ones involved in this crisis. Our four children, who had suffered the loss of the ideal nuclear family dream, had invested their hopes in us. They each wanted home, stability, two parents in love, security. It was an unbearable thought that they should again be denied this. But the unforgivingness and mistrust that smoldered between John and me was at that time an effective deterrent to the blending of these two families into one.

In a way, it was the old "Us against Them" game. Sometimes I found myself mentally positioned to protect and nurture Christi and Juli before Jessica and Matthew. I was less patient and open with Matt and Jessi, and John was less willing to accept the in-house-father role that Christi and Juli needed of him. As John and I concentrated on our own great needs, which we expected and demanded that the other fulfill, we became completely unable to fulfill what was being asked of us. We were stalemated— each demanding, each unable to fill the demands. The stalemate lasted for months.

One night about a year after we were married, I was home alone, and glad of it. The house was quiet. No children asking questions. Nobody needing something washed, ironed, cooked, or found. No squabbles between the kids. No John with whom to attempt an interim truce.

I walked restlessly from room to room fighting back tears, then dragged myself up the long spiral staircase, feeling weighted down with the most profound sense of sadness and defeat I had ever experienced. In our bedroom I lay facedown on the carpet to pray.

This was no night for polite little prayers. I yelled at God, reminding Him of the peace and joy He had visited on John and me on our wedding day. With bitter tears of disappointment, I asked Him if the peace was a trick. Was it something that, after all, couldn't be counted on? I thought He'd been leading me to marry John, and if I hadn't rightly heard His voice about that, then I wasn't sure I would be able to trust my hearing again. *A second marriage break-up? This just can't be happening!*

My agony and inner confusion overwhelmed me. Unable to put words to my despair, I began to pray in my prayer language. (A prayer language captures the intensity of emotion that one cannot find English words to express and becomes the prayer one doesn't know how to pray.) As my prayer language rose in me, I could feel my emotions being caught up in it, being wrung out of me. I began to listen to the words, and I noticed a word I had never heard before. It came again and again, and was finally joined by two other words. My prayer language is one unknown to me, but I can recognize it as the same language by its sounds each time I use it. But these three words were different—I had never heard the Holy Spirit pray them through me before.

They were so distinctly different that I got up and wrote them down.

Shamah
Shala
Shalam

They sounded Hebraic. I wondered just what they might mean. When I prayed them, I felt strengthened, renewed, and hopeful. But it would be over a year before I was given their meaning.

A few days later, I got a phone call from an old friend from whom I hadn't heard since before I left Tulsa.

Mary Taulbert, a dear friend, is one of the most remarkable women I've ever met. I first heard her speak to a group of wealthy Tulsans, who had gathered in a home prayer group. With great confidence, and even greater love, she stood before them and told what it was like to be a mother, poor and black, raising children alone in rural Mississippi. She had begun raising her children in a house so rundown that you could watch the sky roll by as you lay in your bed. She wasn't referring to sky-lights, either, but rather to holes in the roof! She had been so stricken with heart disease that she was dying. The Lord had come to her and healed her. He didn't stop with her body, but healed her circumstances as well. One of her children had already graduated from Oral Roberts University and had become a banker—a miraculous thing for a child from Glen Allen, Mississippi.

That day she had spoken of God's great compassion. Now, four or five years later, she was again speaking of God's great compassion.

"Patti, the Lord told me to call you," she said.

"Mary, after all these years it is so wonderful to hear your voice. How are you?"

"I'm fine, honey. But I didn't call to talk about me. Patti, how is your new marriage coming along?"

It was embarrassing to have to tell her that we weren't doing so well.

"Well, honey, God has told me to call and encourage you. He said that He had sent John to you. John is God's little lamb. He's been badly wounded, and God wants you to love him. Help him get well. Remember, he is God's little lamb. So you take good care of him.

"And don't be worrying about your 'ministry.' Your ministry is just to sit right where you are now. That's your calling—where God's put you. You let Him work in you what He wants to work." Then, without ceremony, she prayed for me and hung up.

I sat stunned as the phone went dead, trying to absorb what I'd just heard. She had never even met John and, apart from prayer, knew nothing about him. In many ways, I didn't want to take it in. I wasn't quite ready to go back to loving John, whatever his needs, or to give up my call to ministry. Yet, somehow Mary's call was linked with the words I'd heard in prayer, words that promised healing and hope. And the call was full of love—her love and God's. What a great love God must have for us both to have sent such a tender message through this dear friend, and how badly we needed to hear the reassurance of His love.

13

Threads from the Past

Patti

elow me, rising from the cloud cover, its craggy face brilliant in the morning sun, was Mt. Hood, an ancient volcano now quiet and peaceful, presiding over the lush Willamette Valley, a temple dedicated to the majestic, creative power of God. To every homebound pilgrim landing at Portland International Airport, it offers a welcoming embrace.

It felt good to be coming home, even though this time the good feeling was tipped with fear.

As my counselor and I had progressed further and further into the core of my feelings, it became evident that, although the problems with John seemed to be the major cause of my anger and disappointment, they could merely have triggered an opening of deeper feelings. She encouraged me to look back into my childhood. But I couldn't remember much of my childhood, and I knew virtually nothing about the histories of those who had raised me. She encouraged me to go back to Oregon and to talk with family, especially with my dad's mother, because she was a person I not only revered and loved, but who also had profoundly influenced my thoughts. I identified more with Granny than perhaps with my own mother.

So I had come back to Oregon to find answers that were somehow hidden not only in my past but also in the histories of my parents and their parents. Unlike calm Mt. Hood, I had within me a volcano that had suddenly become active. I had to find its roots, the source of its strength. What had shifted in the bedrock of my personality to cause this hot flow of rage and terror to spew from my soul?

I thought about the night that had precipitated this trip. The hope that had risen for a moment with the words in my prayer language and from Mary's call had ebbed away. My faith in God's power to fix our situation was eroded by the angry emotions that I let simmer within me. I could not give John the love urged by Mary. All I could see, all I wanted to see, were John's faults—his untruthfulness, his irresponsibility—and the fact that I still didn't have a ministry and that we still had a mountain of debt. A few nights before my departure, all hell had broken loose—again. Crouched up against the headboard of our bed, the sheets gathered up around me like a shield, I screamed and yelled and threatened with all the fury I could muster.

John tried everything he knew to quiet and comfort me. But I would not be stopped. This man, whom I had loved so completely, so fearlessly, was now my enemy, and I hated him. The strength of that hatred, mixed now with a river of tears, frightened us both. I had never loved anyone with such abandonment that the age-old walls of internal protectionism had crumbled. Not until John. In giving all of me into his care, I had lost all of me. The weight of disappointment and feelings of loss had snapped an already frayed cord that had held my inside world together.

John didn't know what to do with me or for me.

The utter futility on his face mirrored the futility in me. The surface me I have known and understood fairly well. But this other Patti who had been uncovered over the months of this marriage, who was both the sum total of all her own life events and surely the depository of ancestral traits, was a mystery to me.

I had to go home. Home to my past. Home to ask questions about my early childhood. Home to my mother and grandmother. To Granny. Surely with all her sense of history and her warm wisdom, Granny could help me unravel those riddles.

Granny hugged me as she always had, right there on the front porch of her little frame house. "Sissy. Darling Sissy. Come on into this house. Dinner is on the table."

Over a dinner of shelly beans, pork chops, fried potatoes, corn bread, and iced tea, I began pouring out my heart. Granny nodded knowingly. Finally I said to her, "Granny, maybe it would help if I knew a little about your past. You know, all of us are made up not only of our own hopes and dreams or joys and loves, but we also carry with us the seeds of thoughts of those who have raised us. I see in your life some of the same struggles I have had to deal with. Can you tell me more about your life?"

She pulled herself fully upright in her chair and looked straight ahead, as if to address the pages of her memories. She cleared her throat and began to speak.

I clicked on the tape recorder I had brought along in the hope that this would happen. I had so much riding on Granny's story, and I didn't want to entrust it all to my memory. Maybe in playing it back again I could find some clues to my own life.

My name is Ophelia Davis Holcombe. I am now eighty-five years old. Five years ago I had a massive heart attack. It was so destructive that the doctors told my children that I could not last through until dawn. I asked the precious Lord to spare my life so that I might have a few years to intercede in prayer for the lives of my children, their wives and husbands, and my many grandchildren and great-grandchildren. He has granted me these extra years to do that very thing. There has been too much pain, sorrow, and confusion in all our lives. I am alive only to pray us all through. And I do pray.

Now let me tell you the story of my life in as true a way as I can. . . .

14

Ophelia Holcombe's Story*
(Birthright of Anger)

Patti

I was born on February 23, 1900, to Levi Davis, a farmer, and Allie Forgy Davis. I was the eighth child in a family of ten, the seventh daughter in this family of nine girls and one boy, all born to the same parents at Baker Springs, Arkansas.

I was a happy little girl at first, as I had a large family to be with. I remember playing so happily with the sisters just older and younger than me. Then Lanie, the older one, got sick, and I have a faint remembrance of her death and how I missed her. I was five and I would cry at night when the loneliness hit me. Just after that, my seventeen-year-old sister, Anna, died. My first memory of Anna was her sweet smile—she was always laughing and making others happy. My mother said many times that Anna's death hurt my father for a long time. Anna helped in the fields where my father worked the crops, and he missed her more than Lanie, who was too small to be in the fields. Lanie was at the house with my mother, and her death hurt my mother dreadfully.

*Compiled from conversations, tapes, and diaries.

My darling mother was patient, understanding, and a very loving person. But she was dominated by my father, never doing anything but what pleased him. Our home was saddened many times by his overbearing ways. His parents had owned plantations and slaves, and when the negroes were freed, the men made slaves out of their women and children, or anyone they could dominate.

When my sisters were old enough to start going with young men, Dad forbade us to go any place for months at a time. When I was four, my oldest sister, Margaret, met her fiancé one Sunday at the house of one of Dad's brothers, and they ran off to get married. The terrible fit Dad had made us all afraid to move or talk. He never let Margaret come back home. In fact, she never came back until after my father died, when our brother was sick. Nor did he let any of us go to Margaret's house, even when her two children were dying. I could see my darling mother grieve over it all. We lived only ten miles from Margaret.

I can't help but grieve over it now to think of what a joy Margaret and her family might have been to my parents, but my dad's terrible domineering ways brought only heartache and pain to all of us, including his brother, who he blamed for Margaret's marriage. They disagreed and quarreled and then quit speaking until my dad passed away.

All my older sisters were home until they were in their twenties. All the courting they did was in letters or seeing their beaux for a short time, always with someone else along.

One day, Dad let Mary, Winnie, Elizabeth, and Henry go to church. While they were gone, he tried to open the girls' trunks to see if he could find any letters. The trunks were locked, so he took a claw hammer and tore the hinges off, ruining the trunks. He found some letters from young men, and oh my! All fury broke loose!

Dad tried to make Mother read the letters, and she cried so hard she couldn't read. I was nine and had been in school three years, so he made me read them; Dad couldn't read or write. Oh dear! What a sad thing for my sisters to come home to. It was terrible for the whole family.

The girls' beaux would bring them to within a quarter of a mile of the house—they knew not to come any farther. When they got to the house, Dad was ready with all the venom Satan could fill him with. He ranted, raved, and threatened to whip them all—two of the girls were over twenty and my brother was twenty! No one could say anything. We were all in tears.

When Dad had these tantrums, he always wound up with a headache that nearly killed him. His face went red as flannel, his neck veins stood out, and you could see his heart beat in them. He would have a tantrum every time he found out that one of the girls had kept company with any of the young men in the neighborhood. Yet, through it all, two more sisters, Mary and Winnie, fell in love and got engaged. Both had to take hard threats and finally wound up getting a hard whipping. But their lovers came and got them as soon as the girls got up courage enough to leave. They loved our home and parents, but knew there was no sense in trying to make peace with Dad and marry at home. So they just picked up and left, risking the chance of never again coming home.

Mary lived close to us and often came to see us when Dad was gone. One summer our well was the only one in the neighborhood that didn't go dry, so Mother asked if Mary could bring her laundry and wash at our well. Dad said yes, but she couldn't come in the house. But one day he told my mother to tell Mary to come in from the wash place. Mary was scared, and we all held our breath, afraid Dad's fury would break out. Instead, Dad met her with a glass of toddy (he always kept whiskey) and was just as sweet as could be. After her first baby came, a boy, no man was ever prouder of a grandchild. It was his first, because he had never let Margaret come home with her children. Mary's second child was another boy, who he also loved. As soon as possible he bought them their first overalls.

In 1911 my mother took a hard chill at her mother's funeral. I remember Mother shaking violently. I'm sure some of it was grief, but I'll never forget how she groaned and suffered. She had to stay at our grandpa's house for a week before she could come home and was never really well again. She passed to her reward six months later. I was eleven.

With Mother gone, nothing was ever the same again. My grandma on my dad's side came to live with us after Grandpa Davis died. There were eight left at home now—Dad, my brother, my grandmother, four sisters, and myself. I learned well in school, but at home I did nothing right for anyone. I loved spelling, reading, or just any of my subjects at school. But when I was fourteen, Dad said I knew all I needed to know, and my older sis sold my books to a schoolteacher.

By then Winnie had married. Dad didn't let her come home for six months, and then he sent word for her to come and get her belongings. When she came he was all smiles, never saying one disagreeable word. A year later Winnie had a son. Dad worshiped his three grandsons. My heart ached for Margaret and her five children, who Dad never recognized.

When I was thirteen, I took Dad's place in the field, plowing with a two-mule turning plow. Dad wasn't very well and would give out easily when breaking the ground for crops.

War broke out in 1914, and Dad worried over that constantly. In November of 1916, my brother Henry went into the Army. While he was gone, Dad had a light stroke. He recovered, though, and early the next year

Henry was discharged from the Army because of a bad elbow. Dad was pleased, but in April 1918, he had a heavy stroke and died about fourteen hours later. We had a very good crop that year, and Henry and I harvested it and put away the hay for the stock, not changing anything we thought Dad would be sorry about.

By the time I was eighteen years old, I had a beau named John Holcombe. I had kept very little company with anyone before my father died because I didn't want to upset him. I could never bring anyone to my home, and if I came part of the way from church with anyone, he was sure to hear of it. I didn't want to be the reason for one of Dad's tantrums and headaches. Besides, I never cared for anyone I kept company with but John. He was my one and only. After Dad died I thought I might keep company with him and no one would care. But I was wrong. Lizzie, my oldest sister still at home, undertook to keep us apart. She said I couldn't get married until she did. I'm sorry to say she didn't have many beaux. She made me go to the kitchen when John came, and I couldn't see him at all, or for only five minutes just before he left to go home.

When John got his call to go into the Army, he came over the last Sunday he was to be home. How it hurt to have to stay in the kitchen and not be with him! It broke my heart, knowing he would soon be going overseas; at that time, soldiers were sent overseas with very little training. My darling was shipped to the front-line trenches in France.

He wrote me every day, and I got the first few letters. But then I didn't hear from him for ever so long. I pined and grieved, wanting to hear, but I never let anyone see me shed a tear. I kept it all hid. Still they could see what it was doing to me.

One Saturday Henry and I went to get the mail. We had to walk two and a half miles, and only went on

Saturday evening, so we could get what groceries we needed as well as the mail. On the way I said to Henry that I hoped I would get a letter. Then I couldn't hold back the tears any longer, but broke all to pieces. Henry cried, too. When we got back to the house, he told my sis, "Lizzie, get the key. Open that trunk. Let Ophelia have her mail, or there's going to be trouble!"

Lizzie had been getting my mail and locking it in a trunk! I was too shocked and hurt to say a word. I had been dominated by her cruelty for so long until it was just best that I said nothing. I could only cry.

Henry died just a year after Dad's death. We were four girls left to keep the farm and the house. Now all the outside work that had been too much for Henry and me to handle together fell to me. A month later John was sent home with an honorable discharge. My heart was still sad about Henry's death, but I felt so full of joy at hearing that my dear John was coming home. But Lizzie still tried to keep us apart. She made arrangements for us not to be at home the first time John tried to come over.

But love true and strong grew between us. Our romance was already in its fifth year in 1919. We saw each other at church every Sunday, though we sat apart. Once in a while he would write a letter and give it to my neighbor, Velma Plunkett, who would pass it to me, and I would do the same. But no letters could go through the mail. It all seems so silly now, but everything that could be done was done to break us up and keep us apart.

On Christmas Day in 1919 I was married at Velma Plunkett's house, because our farm had been sold, and we girls were to go and live with various uncles. John and I stood outside on the long walk leading from the gate to the front door, between two large trees, so green and Christmas-like, to say our vows. After all the good wishes from the neighborhood, we walked into the house to a beautiful wedding dinner, with a nice big turkey, though I could hardly eat a bite. Thank God for the wonderful goodness and kindness of neighbors.

John and I moved into a little three-room house on a farm and started our first year together. We put in a large crop and worked together, as happy as could be.

Our first baby came to John and me the first year of our marriage—a brown-haired, brown-eyed girl. Every two years, the boys came after that. All were sweet and loved. I lost one baby that I carried seven months, until I took typhoid fever. I would have had six boys and one girl if I could have kept him. I had to be consoled by knowing that God knows best and takes care of His own.

After our girl was born, we moved to Plunkett-ville, Oklahoma, and I began eighteen years of waiting on the sick and delivering babies. There is where I found the Lord sweet to my soul. I can't tell you how great it is to know the Lord in the free pardon of sin, unless you've had a similar knowing experience of how to be really saved. I feel like shouting it from the hilltops yet. It's like joy, joy, joybells ringing in my heart. We all went to church, graced our table, had prayer, and had Jesus for our Guide through those eighteen years.

I was kindly known as the country doctor and was called on to nurse people through numerous sicknesses. My sister gave birth one time to an eight-month baby. The doctor said, "Wrap it up, it won't live long," and then told my two neighbors to let it alone. They told me it wouldn't live. But I warmed blankets on my kitchen stove and wrapped that little boy in them. Then I took a little coffee, put sugar in it until it was a syrup, and fed the baby a drop or two at a time, keeping him good and warm by the stove. I worked frantically for five hours, and to everyone's surprise by then he was pink in color and sound asleep—a thing of beauty to look at. How I praised God that after the doctor laid him down to die, I saved his life. Oh, what gratitude I had, to know I could fight in the time of death and win!

Life was hard through the Depression. We sharecropped, and when we harvested our crops, there was never anything left. When we paid for seed, fertilizer, and feed, it took all our money. We always had our garden, and I canned every vegetable. We took our corn to a grist mill to be ground into corn meal. If there was no money for buying flour, we ate corn bread for breakfast. But not for long, because there was always some work my husband could pick up.

Debts always came first. I remember a neighbor who wanted John to sign a note for him, to be paid by a certain time. When the note came due, he didn't have any money, and John got a scary letter telling him to pay off the note, since the neighbor couldn't pay. I had a nice brood sow, given to me when she was a very young pig. My pet was the only way out. So John butchered her to pay off the neighbor's debt. It was the dead of winter at the time, and I was out of shoes. I wrapped my feet in gunny sacks and went out in six inches of snow to hang my laundry. With two babies in diapers, the laundry had to be dried. I want you to know I felt that the man we paid that debt for was as low as a snake, but still we had to keep our debts paid in full. We couldn't let our name be known as one that would never pay a debt, and we raised every child to feel the same way.

15

Granny's Legacy

Patti

ranny stopped, stared out the picture window entwined with years of gangly growth from an old philodendron. Finally, she took a drink of the strong black tea that had been her daily companion for as long as I could remember.

I knew some things that Granny hadn't told me herself. She seemed to have a basic distrust for men, especially those in positions of authority over her. She had suffered many an injury, not only from her father but, I suspect, also from her own beloved John. It turned out that she had married a man whose temperament was like that of her father. It is no wonder that she viewed men as one would view a nuclear reactor—greatly powerful and useful, but extremely dangerous under certain conditions—so best keep some emotional distance as a cushion in case of a meltdown. She feared male domination and had often spoken of not letting a man get the upper hand. Although she became forgiving and mellow in her later years, she was not so in my formative years. Even as a child, I was aware that Granny had been so hurt by men that she was very hard on them, even to the point of manipulating them. Knowing all this helped me understand what Granny said next.

"Sissy, there was so much hurt in my life. It all kind of heaps up over the years. If I hadn't had the help of the dear Lord, I guess I'd a just died. But He did help me. And He will help you. There is no reason why you can't have a full and satisfying life.

"Years ago I asked Him to remove the bitterness and sour feeling in my heart over all of these happenings. Oh how I wish I'd done it earlier. I wasted many a year, many a year.

"Now, honey, the rest of the story you pretty well know. We moved to Oregon after the kids were pretty well grown. Your daddy married your mama, and then he went off to World War II. Then in 1947 you were born."

I clicked off the recorder, and Granny and I laughed and talked a while longer. We both needed the laughter after her intense recapturing of her life.

I hugged and kissed her beautiful old weathered face. It was early spring, and I noticed as I was leaving that her yard, normally so full of daffodils, roses, snowballs, and peonies, had not recovered from the severe Oregonian winter that year. Never mind, by June she would have it beautiful again.

Only that year, June didn't come for her. In April, Granny went to be with the One she had grown to lean on and love so dearly.

Through the trip out to see Granny, the Lord further revealed roots of pain in my life. I thought about that trip a lot, and about Granny's role in my early years.

While I was growing up, I spent many wonderful hours at her house. Even now my mind is full of memories that come flooding back in colorful tidbits: spending the night at her house; watching TV until late in the evening; the bunkhouse-style upstairs bedrooms; the apple orchard and vegetable garden; the white and purple grape vines; the flowering shrubs and beds of colorful perennials.

Through Granny's influence, I gained a love for gardening, for cooking, for nurturing life, for peonies, talcum powder, strong tea, and a hundred other wonderful things. Granny had—as all grannies do—great gifts of life to bestow in her offspring, not only through environmental contact, but also through affinities, attitudes, and genetic strengths and weaknesses that traveled down the bloodline. And along with her wonderful chicken and dumplings and apple cobbler, she also served up a potent plate of fear and accompanying hostility toward men.

My cousins and I absorbed far more than dinner on our visits to Granny's. Today all of my girl cousins who were reared during her time of anger have known rocky relationships, and several of us have known divorce. Perhaps it is coincidental. But perhaps it is the effect of her injury-induced judgmentalism's being visited on successive generations. In fact, if you line up all of her offspring you will notice in our midst a strong showing of physical diseases that have their roots in emotional injury, recurring generation after generation. Arthritis and alcohol abuse are perhaps the most obvious. Failed marriages, broken relationships, and low self-esteem are also apparent.

Granny was truly one of the most loving, giving women the world has ever seen, a saintly woman who will be greatly rewarded by God. Her life was a rich tapestry of sacrificial giving. She fed from her garden and clothed from her faithful sewing machine not only those in need in her family, but also anyone in the little town in which she lived. She nestled us all safe and warm on her ample bosom, and there she sang us her song of life.

It's just that some of her songs contained such killing sadness. She had been badly damaged in her emotions, and the damage went unchecked for a lack of understanding how to heal it. Little threads of sorrow, grief, and anger were twisted into cords of hostility and bitterness that became chains of illness and loss for an entire family. I wondered just how much these "generational sins" were affecting my life and my relationship with my husband. I had long since identified *his* shortcomings, *his* failures in our marriage. As real as they were, were they really so evil and debilitating that I should be feeling that my only alternative was divorce?

How much of our marriage was I seeing through my eyes and how much through Granny's? Was I seeing my husband through the lenses she had given me? Undeniably, he had, by his actions, damaged our relationship. But just how much damage was I doing by judging him so harshly and without mercy? What was keeping me from being able to fully and freely forgive?

It became clear that John and I *both* had an armload of ugly things to take to Jesus.

Though I didn't want to admit it, John was working on his problems. I had watched John trudge up the mountain to present his failures to Christ. Mentally I had whipped him on, saying in my heart, "It's about time you did something about the mess you've made of things."

All the time I was standing on the sidelines quite unaware that while he stood before God clean, I still had business to do with God. If I had been able to see what was really inside my bridal bouquet that day I walked blissfully down the aisle toward John, I would have noticed that hidden among the roses and Queen Anne's lace were little hand grenades of rage, of fear, of brittleness of spirit, and of unforgiveness. Self-righteousness, however, had obscured my vision. John was becoming fresh and pure, while I struggled to contain the effects of the exploding grenades.

16

Overcoming Generational Sins

Patti

*O*n the plane coming home I thought more about the traits in Granny that I could see in myself—the "generational sins" showing up so clearly in her children and grandchildren, and even in her great-grandchildren. The phrase *generational sins* seemed like a long string dangling before my eyes with a sign on it that read, "Pull this."

It was another clue to wholeness on the inside. God had been so loving to both John and me by sending us these clues, revelational breakthroughs to rooms in our pasts, places that had floated around in our subconsciouses, just out of reach of memory. These rooms held real keys to our current actions as well as our reactions. Though we still held on to hurt feelings and fears, we were being blessed with these clues that motioned us to proceed.

I had first heard of generational sins a few months before from two friends, who were also my prayer partners. Trish Hamilton is an accomplished Bible teacher and is in demand all around this area of the country. Jayne Ann Woods had at one time been a member of the governor's cabinet and a tough-as-nails lawyer, but seven years before this she had met the Lord. Some Nashvillians still couldn't get over the changes that had occurred in her. She now pursued God with the same intensity and zealous energy she had once spent on being one of the best lawyers in Tennessee. She was now, like Trish, a student of the Bible and an ardent prayer warrior. She and Trish had teamed up to form a prayer and teaching ministry.

I first met Trish and Jayne Ann during my single years when I had gone to them for prayer. I guess I was expecting that these two ladies, who were so skilled in praying prayers of deliverance, would wear their hair in tightly wound buns at the napes of their necks. Instead, they both looked as if they had just stepped off the pages of *Town and Country* magazine. In addition to their striking physical beauty, they both had serene eyes, joyous spirits, and firm hands in dealing with any representatives of hell that had been sent to disrupt the life of one of God's children.

They didn't ask me many questions before they began to pray, preferring to let the Holy Spirit lead them to the troubled areas He wanted to deal with. In fact, small talk was quietly brushed aside as we three got on with the business of the day. We sat close together, and they began to pray quietly in the Spirit, stopping occasionally to be silent. I could feel the presence of God.

As we each became focused solely on the presence of a wonderful God, everything temporal faded into nothingness. His anointing hung over us like clouds of light and covered the room as if with dense blankets of love. In this atmosphere, Jayne Ann and Trish began to share some Scriptures with me, the basis of the prayers they felt led to pray over me.

Jayne Ann opened her well-worn Bible to Ephesians 6 and started to read aloud at verse 12. "For we are not fighting against human beings but against the wicked spiritual forces in the heavenly world, the rulers, authorities, and cosmic powers of this dark age" (TEV). The passage went on to describe the putting on of the proper equipment to fight such forces. She finished with the 18th verse: "Pray on every occasion, as the Spirit leads. For this reason keep alert and never give up; pray always for all God's people" (TEV).

Then Trish read another verse from Matthew: "I will give you the keys of the Kingdom of heaven; what you prohibit on earth will be prohibited in heaven; and what you permit on earth will be permitted in heaven" (16:19 TEV). With that, she closed the book, laid her hands on my head, and began to pray.

Our session lasted several hours that day, and I left having cried a bucket of tears but feeling renewed, cleansed, and strangely unencumbered. It was the beginning of an awakening to spiritual awareness at a new level for me. The roots of blockages and bondages, the source of many of my problems, were coming into clearer focus.

With their help, I became keenly aware that just as there is a kingdom of light that builds us, blesses us, and perfects us, there is a kingdom of darkness that seeks to take residence in our circumstances, attitudes, reactions, and perceptions, seeking literally to destroy our spirits, minds, and bodies. And, further, these spirits of darkness not only wage war against individuals, but also seek to wipe out entire families, a generation at a time. They inspire tendencies to become patterns, predispositions to become gaping holes in our walls, negative attitudes to become thought patterns so strong that we become chained to the results.

I realized that most people I knew, including myself, had only half appropriated the work of Christ on the cross. We accepted salvation, believing ourselves bound for heaven. But beyond that we often remained victims of a fallen world, victims of grief and tragedy, bent over by disappointment, smoldering in anger at the injustices we experienced, longing to love, to forgive, to be free, but not fully recognizing what inhibits our freedom.

How is it that guilt can retain such a crippling hold on the believer, even after the sin and failure have been taken to the Lord? How is it that anger and unforgiveness can break through the surface like a missile fired from some subterranean silo, even after we have repeatedly asked God to forgive us for that very anger and unforgiveness?

It was at this demonic kingdom of darkness that Trish and Jayne Ann took accurate aim.

As soon as I returned from Oregon, I called them. I wanted to pray about what I had learned—about the sources of anger and stubbornness from my own family. This time they read Deuteronomy 5:9-10: "Do not bow down to any idol or worship it, for I am the Lord your God and I tolerate no rivals. I bring punishment on those who hate and on their descendants down to the third and fourth generation. But I show my love to thousands of generations of those who love me and obey my laws" (TEV).

I related the Scripture to my own situation. In the genealogy of my parents, grandparents, and great-grandparents on both sides, there are instances not only of physical disease and traits transmitted genetically, but also rebellions against the authority of God, a reverence of things other than God. The consequences of these rebellions could be seen in successive generations. Granny was merely one of several ancestors who had input into my physical, mental, and spiritual makeup.

Jayne Ann and Trish bound the works of Satan in John's and my lives. They rebuked and bound and smashed in prayer the many demonic strongholds that were producing such havoc in our lives. They prayed against curses, generational sins, predispositions toward failure, judgmentalism, anger, rage, unforgiveness, procrastination, fear. They covered us both with the precious blood of Jesus and prayed for a vibrantly healthy and fulfilling relationship for us. They prayed for emotional healing in our home and our children. They waded knee deep in the mire of human failure and unforgiveness and waved the banner of the cross over it all.

We did not produce an instantaneous miracle of rebirth for the marriage. But we did begin a process, a peeling back of layer after layer of human frailty and Satanic intervention, as God directed. The three of us, Jayne Ann, Trish and I, began to meet weekly. At each session, it seemed the Holy Spirit exposed places that needed healing. Some reached way back into my childhood. As divine words of wisdom, knowledge, and revelation came, we applied them as tools of effective intercession for my home and marriage. We saw—and are seeing—roots of bitterness and failure pulled out one by one as Jesus wields His sword of the Spirit far more delicately and effectively than the greatest surgeon.

Our sessions of prayer have not only produced great streams of healing in my life, but also have benefited their lives as well, as we have interceded for our husbands and children week after week. We have become bonded together as sisters, carrying one another's loads. Our sessions are like one pillar of a very strong support system being built for me.

As a result, the hopeless marriage was slowly dying and a marriage filled with hope was coming to life.

John

When Patti returned from her trip to Oregon, I saw the hope she brought with her and sensed it was genuine. She had not found any generational scapegoats to blame her own failures on. Rather she now had a framework that helped her make sense of and begin to deal with who she really was down deep. She is uniquely herself; yet, she is also a composite, in many ways, of her ancestors. As are we all.

Encouraged by Patti's search, I, too, looked to my family for clues to understand more of myself. I took advantage of an invitation to attend a father-son banquet with my dad at the Methodist church I had attended the first eighteen years of my life, to spend some time with my parents in Pennsylvania.

The morning after the banquet, I drove with my mom and dad to the graves of my great-grandmother Mamie, and my grandmother Alta. I knew and loved both of these women, but I wanted to know more about them. Mamie was really more like a grandmother to me, because she had raised my mother. Her daughter, Alta, was divorced from her husband, my grandfather, and lived in another town. She came home on weekends to see her mother and daughter. Mom told me of her childhood with Mamie. She spoke of the years of joy, but also of the pain that the divorce brought to her young life. This was at a time when broken homes were not statistics quoted on the front pages of popular magazines, but were quietly whispered about.

Mom also told me about her first date with Dad. He came to the house, all nervous, to ask Mamie's permission to take her granddaughter to the skating rink. When he finally mustered the courage to ask, Mamie said no with a stern face. Dad persisted, and Mamie dug in. She absolutely didn't think it was a good idea.

The three of them sat there in silence for a minute or two. Dad couldn't think of anything else to say. Finally the silence was broken when a song came on the old stand-up radio that had been playing softly in the background.

Put on your nightie and get into bed,
You're not going bye-bye tonight.

Mamie finally cracked into a smile, and the young couple were reluctantly granted a half hour at the skating rink!

As I listened to Mom talk, I was getting a better sense of my heritage and of its strengths and weaknesses as well as a sense of perspective on myself.

I cannot let myself have any license because of the faults of my ancestors. Even though some negative tendencies are genetically mine, my sins and failures are my own. God, however, places a healing stream within each open heart that cleanses us and protects us from the effects of generational sins. Again I find myself in a position of seeming to make a theological point while being anything but a theologian. But to me, the greatest dissertations on God are the changed hearts of His children.

As a Christian, I have a new ancestry—a relationship with God as one of His children. His blood, through the death of His Son, flows mingled with my own. He is love. He is only good. There is no bad in Him to be passed to me. This is where the answers are. I cannot change myself, who I am, but God can. Any weakness, whether it be a predisposition to divorce, anger, unforgiveness, arthritis—whatever one may discover in one's background, can be taken to the cross as it is uncovered. It can be washed in the same blood that forgives the sins we commit by choice. The passing down of brokenness can be stopped right there.

God passes down only wholeness.

I was placed in this world and became part of a family without choice. But I enter God's family by choice and into wholeness by appropriation.

Patti and I were well into the restoration process when we felt the need to find a new church home. We had been attending a wonderful fellowship in Nashville, and while we were satisfied with the depth of spiritual life and teaching, we were dissatisfied with the size of the church. We felt we were being lost in the ocean of thousands of believers that met each week.

Trish had told us about St. Bartholomew's Church—or St. B's as it is affectionately known—an outpost of the Episcopal renewal movement in Nashville. Neither of us knew much about the Episcopal Church and nothing about this particular parish, but Trish's description of the warm mix of formal liturgy and believers' praise induced us to check it out.

Our first visit was, for us, a timely one. I looked around to see what everyone else was doing. Imitating them, I lowered the kneeler softly to the floor. Patti knelt beside me. The man in front of us had his *Book of Common Prayer* open and appeared to know what he was doing. I watched him for cues, not wanting to miss any of the service.

God's presence was very real to us that day. The wonderful balance of liturgy and love was a welcome feeling to two people on the road to being healed, but still very scared. We came back the next week and the next and the next. We were met with open arms and open hearts. God began to show us that, for restoration to continue in our lives, we needed to become a part of a "body," a supporting community, where we could serve and be served.

Here were people who believed in God and practiced what was preached. The youth minister would actually make a date to pick up our children at school and have a soft drink with them, just so he could get to know them. Here was a caring and active counseling ministry. The choir spent as much time praying for others as they did rehearsing. Here were people who went regularly to the prisons and ministered to the inmates. Here was a group who helped feed and clothe the poor. Here were people who were, like us, on the mend from some kind of brokenness, desiring to know God.

We made our home at St. B's. We could come and go without the pressure of sustaining an "appearance" of perfection. We could be ourselves.

We saw the parish as one of God's answers to our prayers for restoration. This was a place of nurturing and accountability. We would not be "Lone Rangers" here. This was to be our family.

17

The Promise of Covenant

Patti

---

*T*he Thermos of coffee was made, and I'd finally figured out something to wear. The hardest part about getting ready for a concert or speaking engagement was finding a whole outfit. (Yes, finally I had been doing a few concerts, both alone and with John.) Lately it seemed that if the dress magically happened to be back from the cleaners, then the shoes needed a trip to the shop for a good polishing face lift. Or if the outfit called for off-white hose, invariably I had a drawer full of gray ones. I always felt a little undone these days and was beginning to identify heavily with Erma Bombeck.

Perhaps the state of my wardrobe was symptomatic of the state of our marriage. It was as though nothing matched any more. When I felt loving toward John, he could only express frustration. But when he would try to be loving, I could only remember his failures and the anger would surge up again. A sustained commitment to wellness and growth still was difficult.

This morning all that I had to be responsible for was one outfit, a couple of cassette background tapes, my notes, and my Bible. And since I was going to the conference alone (the date had been booked before I met John), I didn't have to worry about my emotional state. I kissed John and the girls goodbye and drove out the driveway, headed for the lodge at Fall Creek Falls State Park. A group of singles was having a weekend retreat, and I had agreed to be the afternoon speaker.

As I was speaking, I noticed a woman standing in the back of the room, listening intently to what I was saying. After I finished, she came up to me and introduced herself.

"I'm Debra Martin. Remember that name? We are destined to meet again."

I did remember her name. She had written me a letter in her very distinctive handwriting, and her name had stuck in my mind. (That letter would be one of many she would write in the months ahead. Her letters were always warm, encouraging, and full of hope.) Debra had read *Ashes to Gold* and felt that God had given her an assignment to pray for me.

Debra worked at Precept Ministries in Chattanooga. That is an organization that exists for the sole purpose of grounding God's people in God's Word.

Debra was delighted to hear that I'd remarried, and she wanted to meet John. There was such an exuberance about her, and she was such a warm person that I was curious as to what made her tick. So I invited her to drive over the mountains from Chattanooga to Franklin for lunch one day.

A week or so later, she drove up to Franklin with another teacher from Precept for lunch. At the table, Debra told John and me that she felt the Lord wanted her to offer us her services as a teacher.

John and I didn't quite know what to do with that offer. It seemed a bit odd, since we had just met Debra. We weren't too sure we wanted to study the

Bible with her. But it seemed Debra was inflamed with a divine directive, and so reluctantly John and I agreed to take a course with her. We still desperately needed help, God knew. We had been going through counseling, but somehow we didn't seem to be getting anywhere. We had been in prayer. Perhaps God was urging us toward something more; perhaps some sort of formalized study was what He wanted. We were anxious to experience all of His streams of healing. Now it seemed that the living Word was inviting us into the richness of the written Word.

As we looked over the courses offered by Precept, we finally decided on Kay Arthur's study of covenant, a theme that runs through the whole Bible. Kay is the founder of Precept Ministries.

A couple of months later, Debra arrived at our door, Bible and books in hand, and for months she made weekly trips over Monteagle Mountain, which separates East Tennessee from Middle Tennessee, braving ice, snow, and often two despondent and brooding students. Through it all she remained undaunted and determined.

When she saw the condition of our marriage, Debra was doubly sure that she'd heard correctly from God about teaching us and that the study we'd chosen was God's precise prescription for the disease of heart that was tearing us to shreds.

At the time I couldn't figure out why she kept coming. We offered nothing in return for her efforts. We weren't even particularly great students. But she seemed driven by something beyond our progress, or lack of it. Week after week she opened her Bible and poured out her love.

Finally thin streams of hope began to break through the remaining clouds in our relationship. Every now and then, I'd catch a glimpse of a light so brilliant that I actually found courage to believe God had a perfect remedy for this ailing marriage and that He was imparting within us strength to accept His remedy. Weekly the stream widened, and the light gradually began to displace the darkness of our minds. It was evident that our progress toward wholeness was to include not only intercession and prayers of deliverance, not only being grounded in and responsible to a church body, but also learning God's word regarding marriage.

John

Our marriage seemed to be both the most comforting and the most discomforting of all states. With Patti it seemed that I had already, in these brief months of marriage, swung like a pendulum, back and forth, touching complete happiness on one side and despair on the other. At times, I felt that I couldn't live up to the blending of selves that marriage demands.

If I could have done what I wanted, it would have been for Patti and me to live a life of isolation from the outside world until we found a balance in our shared life. Obviously, this was impossible. We were trying to blend our two families, as well as ourselves, but as musicians and public performers, we had to perform in public.

Patti's fear that I was neglecting her career was unfounded. Some months after we married, she and I began to do concerts together. We started writing and recording a new album on which Patti did the lead vocals and songs, and I did the keyboards and orchestration. We discovered that we liked working together. The result was that we decided that both of us should go out on concert dates, rather than Patti's going out for solo performances, as she had done in the past. If we were, indeed, going to have a shared life, at every point in which our talents and minds could intersect, they should. So at our concerts she would sing, and I would play the keyboards.

What we hadn't counted on was the fact that we couldn't turn the cycles of despair and discovery on and off. There were times when we were really down and in the throes of angry recriminations; yet, we had to sing about God's teaching and cleansing. At other times, the hope that was beginning to seep into our relationship helped us through a concert.

I remember in particular one concert in North Carolina. Patti was singing the song I had written while I played:

> Let the husbands be husbands
> And the wives be wives,
> Let the church preach marriage
> As God-sanctified,
> Each home a small version
> Of Christ and His bride—
> Let the husbands be husbands
> And the wives be wives.*

I knew the song well enough to watch the audience as I played. Their eyes were fixed on Patti, many of them visibly moved. I wondered if they would even have bothered to come if they had known what we said to each other just hours before.

In the motel room before the concert, we went through another time of darkness. A small disagreement had quickly erupted into a major argument. At these times, despair was the norm for us both. The subject of the fight wasn't important enough for us to remember, but I can still feel the impact of the words and the sting of the silences. We were good fighters! If

*"Husbands and Wives" by John and Patti Thompson. © Copyright 1984 by Morning Gate Music, Life Gate Music, and Day Spring Music. Used by permission.

sharp words were ammunition, then that motel room was an armory.

I wanted to call the pastor of the church and say we couldn't come to the concert. It would have been easier for me to go up on the platform and say to those people, "Please forgive us, but we have nothing to say to you," than to confront our problem head-on.

But somehow we knew we had to. The weeks of sitting in the enclosed sunporch, studying the biblical teaching of covenant, had planted truth in our spirits that could not be avoided or rationalized away. It just had to be faced.

How could the story of Abraham, an ancient desert nomad walking between the dead parts of a sacrificed animal, have any truth relating to me, here in a small rented room with a broken air conditioner and a furious wife?

Somehow it did. I began to understand that God's view of our marriage was not the same as mine. I was in a covenant relationship with Patti *and* with God. There were three of us involved here. My words to her on our wedding day went far beyond the pledge of my love or even the injury I felt as a result of this argument. My responsibility to her was of primary importance to God and to me.

A covenant is a binding agreement. A contract. An unchangeable promise. Abraham had entered into a covenant with God. God told him to bring the required animals, cut them into pieces, and walk between the pieces. What this said to me was that I must walk into death. Here, in this room, I was to die to the pride and ego that blocked me from communicating with and loving my wife, my covenant partner. How contrary to the world's system of values, and to my own past, was this way of living.

While studying covenant, I read in Ephesians 4:22-24 that I was to put off my old self and be made new in the attitude of my mind—to put on a new self, created to be like God. That was difficult in the midst of this motel scene, because it meant denying my right, even my right to be right.

But I began to understand how God viewed His covenant, and my life began to change. The exits I had so easily taken before when faced with a painful confrontation were now blocked, not by a set of harsh rules, but by an example of love so strong and compelling that I could not get around it.

In Ephesians 5, I read the hardest, most difficult words I could imagine, not the often-quoted, "Wives, submit to your husbands," but the quieter, "Husbands, love your wives as Christ loved the church." This commandment, coupled with a beginner's under-standing of covenant, was the foundation that I was to build on. Christ loved the church so much that He gave his life for her. She is His bride—the object of His adoration and sacrifice. He is her Savior, the one who saved her from all danger, evil, and from the damage she could do to herself.

It was still very difficult for me to love Patti as I should. In my stubbornness I would have preferred to become very quiet and shut Patti out, taking comfort in the fact that I was not understood and loved the way I should be. I would have preferred not to spend my self-preservation on her. But that night in North Carolina, I walked across the small desert we had created in that motel room, and we prayed together. I was taking God at His word, and I wanted Him—and Patti—to be able to take me at mine. This was covenant, not merely theory or theology. Nor was it some rigid Judaic marriage encounter. It was the joy of a promise experienced at the life-changing level.

My marriage was an act of covenant. God viewed it as such. I was learning to. I was to love Patti as Christ loved the church. The "fleshing out" of these truths had to begin somewhere. That day I saw that the "somewhere" was with me. I had to take that huge first step in being to Patti what my Example was and is to the church, His bride.

That step was to bring a new sense of freedom to me. There was much, much more to learn about the mysterious beauty of our "promise." But this was about all I had the courage to deal with in North Carolina. We had forever to live up to the rest of the contract. Forever.

> Each home a small version
> Of Christ and His bride—
> Let the husbands be husbands
> And the wives be wives.*

As we finished the song I watched the audience again. A few of the older couples nodded in peaceful wisdom that I knew had come from discoveries far beyond our own. Others seemed to be at the same point in the journey. Some were desperate; some were bored. God was with us all.

Would it be possible for us—two people from such scarred, broken pasts, two people with flaring self-pride, self-interest, two people with a collection of excess baggage brought with them into this relationship—would it be possible for us to actually blend our hearts and become as one? And to blend our families?

We could see by what was now unfolding in our lives that, indeed, it was possible. In spite of our failures in loving each other, love was surviving. For this reason, our marriage would succeed and blossom and be beautiful when some others with, perhaps, fewer problems would fail.

*"Husbands and Wives." © Copyright 1984 by Morning Gate Music, Life Gate Music, and Day Spring Music. Used by permission.

We saw that, without any doubt, we could (and should) trust God. We could trust not with a passive assent that merely nodded to the truth that God is, but with an aggressive affirmation of its relevance:

God is *love*. Therefore, enveloped in His love, our love would survive.

PART III

"I know that whatever God does endures for ever"

Ecclesiastes 3:14

Grace

And there is a miracle that
must be penned about how
he and I have been healed.
No, not cancers melted, or
inches added to limbs, but
that to these embarrassingly
impudent, religious sinners,
God's costly grace revealed.

P.T.*

18

The Pain of Being a Long-Distance Parent

Patti

S pringtime in Tennessee is, for me, the epitome of what the Creator intended it to be. After a gray and often bitterly cold winter, spring has become utterly necessary to our survival. We simply cannot bear another day of gray, and the whole state seems to be holding its breath during the last days of cold. When the first crocus pops us, you can hear a collective "whoopee" echo from Memphis to Knoxville. We know that crocuses are followed soon by tulips and daffodils, which local residents call buttercups, early magnolias, and pink and white dogwoods.

As soon as we have a few warm days, we start our gardens and begin to move living rooms to porches and patios. From out of attics and basements come the wicker rockers and settees, the folding chairs and chaises, and from our living rooms and kitchens come our houseplants to catch the sun. Out come the neighbors, fireflies, and iced tea. John often says that the ills of American society cannot be solely pinned on the likes of drug pushers, porno kings, or headline-hungry media, but architects must take some of the blame as well, because they have almost ceased to include wide and inviting porches in their contemporary designs. Families have no space to wander after supper, iced tea glasses in hand, for talk uninterrupted by TV or radio; there is no place to sit and wave to the young neighbors pushing baby strollers and older citizens taking their daily constitutionals.

Fortunately, the old section of Franklin, Tennessee, has largely been spared too many modern "improvements." We still have our fine porches, our wicker furniture, and our iced tea.

Late on a beautiful Friday afternoon in 1984, John and I headed north into Nashville, watching the spring sunlight turn the newly sprouted fields into a magical, luminous green that cannot be duplicated in pictures or paintings. We reveled in the beauty of the Tennessee landscape and looked forward to the weekend with Matt and Jessi, whom we were going to pick up.

They were waiting on their front porch with their weekend bags packed, we hoped, with their Sunday clothes as well as games and toys. We always had to check to see if Matthew had his sports jacket and dress shoes. Many were the Sundays we frantically looked under all the beds for loafers left behind in Nashville!

"Hi, Daddy. Hi, Patti. Boy, do we have an announcement," Matt said as he threw his bag into the back of the station wagon.

"Daddy, we're moving to Alaska! In July."

Suddenly, the beauty of spring vanished.

John

Our dinner that night was much quieter than usual. When we had finished and the children had gone outside to play, I asked Patti to take a walk with me. On the familiar streets of Franklin, where we had begun our life together, I was able to tell her the hurts and confusion that I couldn't seem to talk about in any other place, particularly about how I loved my children and how it hurt to be away from them so much.

As we walked, I would tell her about Matt and Jessi's early years, before she knew them. Each store-front we passed seemed to trigger another story. A pair of ceramic ballet shoes in a craft store window made me think about Jessi's birthday three years before.

It was her sixth, and that year it fell in the middle of the week. She and Matt were living with their mother, who agreed to let me take the children out for an early dinner to celebrate. I had told Jessica that she could go any where she wished. For a week she considered all the options, and a few days before the special day she phoned to tell me her choice.

"The morning of her birthday I woke up alone in my house," I told Patti, "remembering the birthdays of my childhood. My mother would come in and wake us with our own private serenade of 'Happy Birthday.' It hurt not to be able to go into Jessi's room and wake her with a serenade. Instead, I sat on the edge of her bed and sang to the two dolls and a teddy bear, who were still positioned exactly as they had been left the last weekend. And just before school time I called Jessi and sang to her over the phone.

"After school let out, I picked them up and drove to my house, where we had cake and presents in a decorated dining room. Then we had supper at McDonald's on West End Avenue beside Centennial Park, just as Jessi had planned. After her favorite meal, we drove into the park up to the Parthenon.

"By this time, it was dusk, and the spotlights were trained on the Parthenon. I got my guitar out of the car, and Jessi brought her ballet bag. We climbed the steps until we stood between the huge columns, in the spotlights. Jessi put on her ballet shoes and a small tutu, and as I played the guitar she danced and pirouetted under the bright lights.

"I watched her dance—a small, graceful girl responding to the grace and beauty of a magnificent building—with a lump in my throat and a heart full of thanks for having been given a moment like this.

"But, oh Patti, what am I going to do? How am I going to make it without them? Who'll watch her do pirouettes on her next birthday?"

As we walked back to the house, I was silent. It hurt too much to talk. All I could think was that I had such little time to prepare for this separation. I guess even if I'd had years I wouldn't have been ready for July 25 to arrive.

I battled with God.

I made deals with God. "I'll do anything if you'll just make it possible for them to stay."

I begged God.

Finally, I bowed, half in submission and half with the bending that comes from a load too heavy to carry.

I had been learning, through the study of covenant, that God never requires from us what He doesn't make provision for. In our marriage, those ancient concepts of dying to self were becoming a part of our daily lives. They were foundation blocks on which we were building our home. But what did God expect from me now? Dying was one thing, but living with the constant pain of separation was another. I might submit, but I would also ask why—why did my lessons in trust have to be so graphic?

Although restoration was beginning to take shape in our lives, we were living through the painfully real consequences of the failures of each of our previous marriages. For me in the next few weeks, that meant living with the prospect of being separated from Matthew and Jessica for nine and a half months of every year. I would gladly have stood in water up to my neck with a fake rifle over my head rather than face this further wrenching apart of our family.

Did God really care? I wondered. How many thousands of fathers silently bear the pain of being a long-distance parent?

As I continued to argue with God, I remembered a song I had written almost a decade ago. As the words and music played in my mind, it suddenly struck me: *God, himself, became a long-distance parent. God required it of himself!*

> That night in all of heaven
> There wasn't a sound
> As God and the angels
> Watched the earth.
> For there in a stable
> The Father's only Son
> Chose to give himself
> Through human birth.
> And when the cry of a baby
> Pierced the universe,
> Once for all,
> Men were shown their worth.*

God had been where I was. He had watched His child leave His home and go to be part of another family. His Son had had a *step*-father. Here was a foothold, or perhaps a handhold, something to grab onto.

Somehow, it was easier now to believe that God does not require what He does not provide for. That truth became another foothold, a place on which to stand.

Matthew and Jessica spent their last month in Tennessee with Patti and me and Christi and Juli. We

*"That Night" by John Thompson. © Copyright 1976 by Paragon Music Corp./ASCAP. All rights reserved. International copyright secured. Reprinted by special permission of The Zondervan Music Group, Nashville.

had never been all together for that long at one time, and it was glorious. But when they left on July 25, I felt as though I had been cut open and part of me stolen. I cried until the place that tears come from was dry. And then I cried tears I never knew I had—dry, heavy tears.

God did not reach an unseen hand through space and set Matthew and Jessica's plane back down, as if it were a toy. But in a greater miracle and act of love, He stood with one man who hurt. It was as if He said, "Trust me to give it all back to you, to restore the lost years. Trust me with the tender places of your heart. Trust me with your most beloved treasures."

This was no Bible study; rather it was the truth of trust written on a weeping heart. *Covenant*—bold, real, and daring—minus any theological trappings. Reality to be counted on.

19

"El Shaddai"

Patti

*L*ife didn't stop after July 25. Our marriage relationship kept growing. And as with all real growth, we experienced the highs and joys that come when love breaks through and asserts its reality. We also experienced the lows that come from the exposure of inner problems that still need to be healed.

John busied himself with his music in the first few months after Matt and Jessi left. At times it seemed that his heart was overworked and must surely break, because in addition to his grief over the loss of the children was the daily challenge of his marriage to me. Undeniably we were making great strides forward in our ability to accept and forgive each other in love. The great welts we had inflicted on each other's heart were losing their puffiness and redness. Yet, as I said, there were lows.

I was still struggling with John's management of our finances. It seemed that consistently effective management was a bit like riding a mechanical bull turned too high and fast—very difficult. John still struggled with my inability to forgive him completely, with no strings attached. He needed my unconditional love and forgiveness. I so wanted him to have it.

But John couldn't escape the fact that God expected his handling of finances to reflect His righteousness just as surely as God expected my forgiving heart to reflect His nurture, unencumbered by judgmentalism. God had revealed himself to Abraham as the God of covenant: El Shaddai. "Walk before me and be perfect—without blame," God had said to Abraham. He said the same thing to me about my heart. He said the same thing to John about finances.

In our own strength, we couldn't do it. Here, too, we had to trust that the God who called us to righteousness would enable us to untangle it all. There was nothing for us to do but face up to our debt and our inner needs—and *trust* that the God to whom we had offered our lives and hearts and assets (talents and fiscal) would somehow be our sufficiency. It seemed that everywhere John and I turned, God made efforts to show us His character.

John

It was a middle-of-the-night melody that played itself over and over in my head until I had to get out of bed and play it on the piano.

In the dark I sat on the bench in my pajamas, the brass pedals cold on my bare feet, and let my fingers define what I had heard in my head. It was a simple melody; yet, there was a strength and wonder to it that defied the simplicity. As the song left my inner world, filling the room, I heard it with my ears and knew that it was a song about God Almighty. It was as if the first three notes were a musical equivalent to His spoken name.

That middle-of-the-night melody soon became the well-known gospel song, "El Shaddai," for which Randy Scruggs and I had received our Dove awards in 1983.

Now, a year or more after my receiving that award, Patti and I were convinced that God wanted to say more on the subject of His Almightiness. Shortly after our marriage, we wrote and recorded "The Anthem of Light" on the album *Hope of the Heart*. That song, too, seemed to fall out of the sky and onto my keyboard. When I played the melody for Patti, she said she knew only one biblical passage that could accurately translate this music into words: Revelation 4:8. It is a description of what is being proclaimed constantly, both day and night, before the throne of God. Heavenly beings are saying: "Holy, holy, holy, is the Lord God Almighty, who was, who is, and who is to come" (TEV).

In the months following Matt and Jessi's departure, Patti and I started to write a musical based on the name *El Shaddai*. We began to do research on the names of God and this name in particular.

The scholar whose notes we studied stated that the name was first given to Abraham by God Himself as an expression of His character. This descriptive name enabled Abraham to know with whom he was dealing and what he could expect—nurturing, provision, shelter, safety, strength, promise. Some scholars believe the name expresses the mothering nature of God and translate it as "the breasted one"—God with breasts full of milk, ready to suckle all who come for food, comfort, and shelter, as a mother takes her children into her arms. Nearly all scholars believe that, while we can determine aspects of the name, we do not know its full meaning; it remains mysterious and undefinable.

When God told Abraham that He was El Shaddai, He added, "Abraham, walk before me and be blameless." It was as El Shaddai that He made the covenant with Abraham and gave the promise that Abraham and Sarah would have a son from whom a mighty nation would spring and whose home would always be the land of Canaan, in which Abraham was only a wanderer. The promise was made nearly two thousand years before Christ came; yet two thousand years after Christ it still stands as a valid contract, a promise that spans centuries, a never-ending promise.

In our research, Patti and I discovered that the name nearly vanished from use. The prophet Ezekiel was the last to use it, when he reported seeing in a dream the glory of El Shaddai leaving the Temple in Jerusalem, then leaving the Hebrew nation (Ezekiel 10 and 11).

Our next discovery stunned us. If Revelation had been written in Hebrew instead of Greek, we read, the name El Shaddai would have appeared in Revelation 4:8! And, therefore, in the song we had written together. It was as if we had been given clues to a great and wonderful mystery. What was God trying to tell us? The picture was gradually coming into focus.

There it was. The Lord, El Shaddai, had given me the song "El Shaddai" at a time when I so needed to hear from Him.

The Lord, El Shaddai, had let me meet Patti on the night I was given the Dove award for "El Shaddai."

The Lord, El Shaddai, had given Patti and me a song together, calling us to worship Him as the All-sufficient One.

The Lord, El Shaddai, had given us the study of His covenant, through Debra Martin, at a point when our marriage desperately needed healing.

The Lord, El Shaddai, was giving us encouragement and inspiration to further explore what He was telling our generation about His character, provisions, and expectations.

And He was speaking to us personally of His promises. He was telling me, just as He had told Abraham, "John Thompson, I am El Shaddai. Walk before me and be blameless." In the middle of all that transpired in my life, God called me to righteousness—me, with my failures, weaknesses, and broken places. El Shaddai was calling me to a righteousness that He would supply.

We were wonder-filled at all we discovered of our God and excited about sharing our discoveries through the musical. Yet, underneath the excitement was still the pain of my children's absence. Creating and putting together the musical took months, months that went by very slowly in spite of the joy and challenge of the music. Finally, it was November, and I was flying to Alaska.

20

Oh, Alaska, Cradle My Babies in Your Arms

John

$\mathcal{T}$he air was cold when I felt Alaska for the first time. The flight had been a long one—Nashville, Dallas, Portland, Seattle, Anchorage. The view during the 6:30 P.M. landing was breathtaking; one side of the plane was in the light, the other side was dark. As I learned in the ensuing days, the Alaskan sky is big enough, on both ends of the day, for darkness and light to be seen at the same time.

It was fully dark by the time I got my bags and rented car, and drove to the motel to check in. The first thing I did was call Patti. Then I called the kids. Their stepfather answered, and I heard Jessica in the background give a joyous yell, "Daddy," when the caller was identified. How good it was to hear Matt and Jessi's voices without the long distance hum we had become accustomed to. We talked about plans for meeting the next morning, and then we had to say goodnight. It was tough to know that I was in the same town as the kids, but couldn't see them until the next day.

Although it was getting close to 11:00 P.M. by Nashville time I was too excited to sleep, so I drove around the downtown area. Anchorage was larger than I had anticipated. It seemed kind of *eskimopolitan*—a blend of old and new, native and imported. There were many obviously new buildings, mostly banks and real estate offices, and several of them used concrete and geometric designs on their edges and corners. There were many computer and video tape stores—for dealing with the long winter nights. There were massage parlors and churches; I was surprised at how many churches. The spirit of the town felt good.

I finally managed to get about two and a half hours of sleep, and at 5:30 I was up and out for the fifteen-mile drive to Eagle River, where Matt and Jessi lived. The plan was that I would pick Matt up at school during his morning break, then bring him back for the rest of his morning, while I had a conference with Jessica's teacher. Then I would pick the children up after their morning sessions. So I was far too early, but I couldn't sit still in the motel.

Eagle River is a new town, with homes scattered throughout the woods on either side of streets. It didn't take long to drive through it or to locate the children's house and school. I had over three hours to spend, so I found a cafe in the center of town, trying to calm the anxiety and anticipation that threatened to overwhelm me.

Finally it was time. As I drove up to the school, I could see Jessi looking out the window. She came running to greet me, but she was so in control of herself it was as though she, or I, had been gone only a few days. Yet I could feel her love as she jumped in my arms, her arms hugging me tight. She had new bangs with her long hair and looked great, adorable, older. Then Matthew came running out of another door, a Matthew with braces on his teeth, looking like a teen-ager. But we still hugged each other hard. He looked healthy, but vulnerable, going to be handsome.

Jessica seemed content to go back to her class after that short break. Mattew had a longer time, so we went for a short drive and talked about everything, Patti, his school, my new curly hair, his friends, Juli, Christi. Then it was time to take him back for the rest of his morning session. For me, it was more waiting.

When I came back to pick the children up, Matt introduced me to two of his friends, charming and articulate young ladies. They wanted my autograph, because of the song "El Shaddai," and then shyly asked if I would play it for them on one of the school pianos. Matt was proud, I could tell. Then Jessi's teacher asked me to play "El Shaddai" for her class.

Finally, it was time to drive to the house to pick up the children's clothes and skis for the weekend. When I'd driven by it earlier that morning, I had been shocked at how small the house was. But it was cozy on the inside, and their stepfather planned to add on to it. The kids showed me their rooms; my cards written to them hung on their walls.

Then, finally, we were *alone* together in the car. I gave the kids twenty dollars each, gifts from Grandma T. and Patti. Matt immediately spent half of his on GI Joe treasures he had been wanting. Thrifty Jessi, as usual, decided to wait and think about it.

At lunch I couldn't stop drinking in the sight of the children—the sweetness in all the little normal, every-day actions and activities. Back at the motel, they unpacked, and I even helped Jessi put her things in a drawer; I think it gave me a sense of permanence.

We spent the rest of the day in the motel, talking or watching TV from the bed, I in the middle, Jessi on the left, Matt on the right, each in a crook of my arms, treasuring every possible moment together. I had a cassette for them of Patti's and my new album, and we listened to it on Matt's cassette player—he was, as always, well equipped.

Finally, about midnight, Jessi gave in to sleep. But Matt and I lasted until about 2:00 A.M. with the help of a funny late-night movie.

We ate breakfast in the room Saturday morning, or at least they did, while I watched them. It was so beautifully and painfully familiar. We were going to go skiing, but first we had to figure out what to spend their money on. Jessica finally decided on her big purchase, a tape by the GoGo's, an all-girl band, with the words to the songs printed on the fold-out cover. She sang along in pitch with every song. And Matt found his find of finds—nunchuks, Japanese warrior things used by the Ninja he had studied about.

After lunch, we went back to the room for a rest. While Jessi sang with her tape and Matt practiced martial arts moves in front of the mirror with his nunchuks, I took a peaceful nap, knowing they'd be there when I woke up.

When I woke up it was practically dark. We went out to see a movie and to buy some things to eat in the motel room. On the way back Jessi got very quiet. "What's wrong?" I asked.

"The time is going too fast, Daddy."

We heated the pizza in the kitchenette that came with the room and talked about what they wanted to do when they grew up. Matt wants to be a part of Thompson and Son! Jessi said, "I want to live wherever you are." I hugged her. In fact, we hugged at every opportunity all through that day.

And then it was Sunday morning. We ate breakfast in the room and then just were lazy in bed for a while, talking with our arms around one another. This time it was Matthew who said, "The time is going too fast, Dad."

"I know" was all I could choke out.

I hadn't been able to find any skis for myself, but we decided to go cross-country skiing up at Hatcher's

Pass, and I would help Jessi learn on her skis. The farther up into the mountains we got, the more snow we encountered and the streams were frozen more solidly. The mountains were magnificent in rugged splendor. The last ten miles of the road were rugged, winding, and steep, with snow on top of gravel—a bit of a challenge for the rented car.

Matt did well at skiing, and so did Jessi. I would catch her when she got to going a little fast. We kept going up and down, up and down. It was exhilarating. At one point, I fell in a small stream bed, breaking the ice and getting wet up to the knees. Fortunately, my boots kept the water out, so only the eight inches of jeans above their tops froze!

It was getting dark at 4:30, so we headed back to Anchorage, the end of the visit staring us in the face. While Matt watched football in the motel room, Jessi and I made an excursion to the grocery store for supper, deciding on hot dogs and buns with cheese, cookies, and milk and Pepsi. While I heated dinner, we phoned Patti so the children could visit with her.

By now the comments of "I wish we had more time" were quite frequent. Whoever said it was immediately comforted by the other two with our by-now-familiar-and-rational response: "We're lucky to be together . . . we're all happy . . . we all love each other . . . we'll always be family." But nothing could take away the pain of impending separation.

We tried to drown it by watching a funny movie. We laughed at it and at one another, savoring the laughter and the company.

Finally Matt and Jessi fell asleep while I watched. I dozed fitfully, but kept waking up to memorize another expression or position. Matthew's cheeks turn different shades depending on how hard he is sleeping. Jessica's sleeping is acrobatic. Once she fell off the bed and slept kneeling with her head on the bed!

And then it was time to get up. The children's school starts very early in the morning, and we had to drive into Eagle River. The children ate a bite of cereal, while I did most of the talking. I was thankful for their love. It was so real. Though I was sad, I also had God's great peace in my heart, and I sensed the children felt it, too. We are not immune from pain because we are Christians. Theoretically, things can always be worse (not a very comforting thought); yet, I know that the difficult moments we endure are the times we learn grace at the heart level.

While the children packed their belongings, I assembled Matthew's dirt bike that I had brought from Nashville in pieces in one of my synthesizer cases. He is a confirmed dirt-biker, and this bike was his favorite. He looked forward to using it on his favorite trails.

We got Matthew to school by 7:00, but since Jessi didn't have to start classes until 8:00 she and I had hot chocolate and coffee at a restaurant. I told her about the new home Patti and I were buying and drew her a floor and yard plan. She would share a room with Juli when she came, and she wanted to know what it looked like. As we talked, she kept telling me that she loved me.

It was still dark when I dropped her off at school. I sensed how difficult life must be during the winter, operating with such few hours of daylight.

I had to make two trips between Anchorage and Eagle River to get all the kids' stuff back to the house. Then it was time to pick Matthew up and half an hour later Jessi, for our last meal together at a local restaurant. We ate slowly, savoring our time together and one another and talking a bit about Christmas.

Now it was getting down to the wire. Jessi had a gymnastics class at 2:00, and while she was at school Matt and I drove up into the mountains behind Eagle River, where he showed me some of his bike trails. Now I had images of them and their surroundings to remember after I left. I can visualize them at home, at school, on their bikes, or walking out on the ice on Fire Lake.

I was to have had one more time with Jessi to say goodbye, but when I got to school, the teacher said that the class had started late and it might be forty-five minutes or so before it finished. I had a plane to catch, so I had to miss those last few moments with her. Matt suggested I go into the class to say goodbye, but I couldn't—it would be hard for both of us in front of her classmates.

So I opted to write her a note. Matt asked if I would write him one, too, that he could read after I'd left. I told Jessica I was proud of her, that she was turning into a beautiful little girl, and that above all I loved her and would always be her daddy. I told Matthew that I was proud of him, that he was my "main man," and that I dearly loved him.

While I was writing, Matt wrote a note for me to put in my Bible and read on the plane. Then it was time to take him back home. As I bent over to hug him, I felt part of my soul rip away.

"I love you," he said, and for the first time ever, I could get no words out to reply. But I knew that he knew.

He was out-braving me this time, although when he saw my tears, he began to cry, too. We walked backwards from each other, he to his porch, I to the car, never losing eye contact. Then we gave each other the old thumbs up, as was our custom. Suddenly he ran back out to me with his Lone Ranger's horse, the horse that had first been a Christmas gift to me in 1958 and which I had given to him when he was four. It was one of his prized possessions. "Put it in my room in Nashville," he said.

As I drove away, the tears streaming down my face, I

prayed and thought about what Patti had said on the phone to me about grief and God's grace.

Sometimes I live for the day when all will be more normal, when the children are in college and come home for vacations, or when they live closer—when I can feel like a normal parent. But God calls me to be their dad *today*, in all I do, even though physically we are apart. Sometimes the wound opens inside and I can't take the pain. I'm learning though to look to God, to ask His forgiveness for the times I give in to grief and take my eyes off Him. I love them so dearly and am deeply thankful for them. God has done a great thing by blessing me with all my kids—Matt, Jessi, Juli, Christi—and my wife, Patti. I'm learning. Light overcomes darkness. Love conquers all.

As I got off the plane back in Nashville, I experienced peace. Not a surface peace, or even a reprieve from the pain of separation from the children, but a peace somewhere deep, beyond understanding, beyond myself. As Abraham had to put the life of his son in God's hands, so I had to put Matthew and Jessica in God's hands. My altar was not a pile of stones on some ancient mountain in Israel. It was in a small suburb of Anchorage, Alaska.

That night I lay awake, overwhelmed with contradictory emotions—the joy of coming home to a loving welcome, and the emptiness of leaving two large parts of myself in Alaska. Patti had fallen into the rhythmic breathing of a deep sleep several hours before and didn't stir when I got up and went downstairs to the piano. I played songs without melodies and prayed prayers without words. I had trusted God before, but the cost had never been so great.

In the flood of prayers and melodies that ran through my head, I singled out one of each that seemed to fit. Suddenly Patti was standing there. "What's that?" she asked. I played for her the short chorus I had written.

> Oh, Alaska,
> Cradle my babies in your arms.
> Oh, Alaska,
> Promise me that you'll keep
> Them safe and warm.
> And every now and then
> On a lonely Tennessee night,
> Would you let me see the glow
> Of your northern lights,
> Just so I'll know
> That they're all right.
> Oh, Alaska.*

21

Trusting the God of Covenant

Patti

*J*ohn returned to us with his heart limping. I was at once compassionate and jealous. As a parent I could identify with the hurt I would feel if I were separated from my children for nine or ten months at a time. But my compassion couldn't comfort John, because it came packaged with jealousy. I felt threatened because my love for him couldn't reach into the room that held his fatherly longings. I was jealous of the part of his heart that seemed to exist outside of our marriage.

John wasn't giving me this grieving part of him. But I wasn't whole enough to accept John as he was. The wife who demands the totality of her husband's heart is clearly not yet in a state to accept even that which is offered. Unfortunately, I didn't know that my "demand" and his loss and consequent brokenness couldn't mix. Grudgingly I thought of grief as his mistress. So when John needed to grieve for his children, he closed himself off from me and went into that place of sorrow alone. I wanted to be included, not so much to bear or share the weight of loss, but that my presence in his heart would not be eclipsed by his loss and grief. As I saw it, love for me and grief over his children vied for first place.

I was still defining love in terms of my need to be made whole by it, not by my willingness to be broken or to die—"except a seed fall into the ground and die, it abides alone," Jesus told us. I had spent so many years struggling to live I didn't want to hear of death. When you get right down to it, love always means dying—I guess that's why most people prefer romance over love.

It seems to me that it is quite impossible to give all of one's heart in marriage if part of it holds bitterness, guilt, hatred, jealousy or other blackening emotions. The heart that provides a haven for these emotions cannot be shared fully with God or another individual, so it languishes in aloneness, further compounding its sorrow.

In spite of the presence of grief, we continued our work together and plunged with renewed vigor into the research and writing of *El Shaddai,* the musical. In the next few months we visited a local Jewish temple, met the rabbi, talked to the cantor, and used the library at the Jewish Community Center in Nashville.

Then for one whole weekend, Dr. Ronald B. Allen, professor of Hebrew Scripture at Western Conservative Baptist Seminary in Portland, Oregon, came to Nashville to share his knowledge of the Scriptures with us. We set up a classroom with a blackboard in the recording studio in our basement and studied every reference to the name *El Shaddai* in the Old Testament, as well as the inferred references in the New Testament.

Dr. Allen's command of biblical Hebrew is not only articulate, but is also warmed and made applicable by his great love for God. It was thrilling to learn from him, and also to find that impressions or thoughts that the Holy Spirit had given to us previously had historical and biblical authenticity.

During our weekend study, I remembered the three words that came to me months before, when, face down, I had cried out to God for help. The words had sounded Hebraic then, and I thought that perhaps Dr. Allen might recognize them: *shamah, shala, shalam.*

When I repeated them for him, his response was both fascinating and frustrating: "Hmmm, what an interesting coupling of words! So poetically tied together. I don't believe I've ever heard those three words used exactly that way. Very poetic—poetic indeed!"

So my words did have a verifiable meaning! I wanted to hurry Dr. Allen out of his appreciation and into translation. Finally, he started to explain their meanings.

"*Shamah.* Well, the first meaning that comes to me is 'to there,' as in location, as in 'in that place, there.'

"*Shala* means 'to be at rest,' or 'to prosper,' or 'to be quiet.' It speaks of completion and peace.

"*Shalam* is the root word for *shalom*, which means 'peace.' It has a much broader meaning than *shalom*, however. *Shalam* speaks of everything as it ought to be, everything as it originally was meant to be, total and complete. It also means sound, whole, and right."

I was overwhelmed and speechless. Nearly a year before this study, God gave me three words in my prayer language that not only sounded Hebrew but were Hebrew. And then He sent an eminent Hebrew scholar to teach us the wonder of God's ancient name, *El Shaddai.* This man also was able to tell me the meaning of the words God had given me. It was such a precious miracle, so personal, so filled with fatherly love and comfort.

"If you were to hear those words together as one thought," I finally asked Dr. Allen, "would they mean, 'There, in the place where you are, is rest, restoration, prosperity, quietness, completion, and there in that place God will make all things as He intended them to be, 'sound, whole, and right'?"

"Yes, Patti," he replied. "According to definition, those words would mean that."

There was God's word of promise to me, His word of blessing. A promise first spoken by the presence of His peace on our wedding day. A promise repeated in our studies of covenant. A promise amplified by the revelation of who El Shaddai is. And now spoken plainly in the meaning of the words of my prayer language.

God was giving us one message through three different media—the research for and writing of the musical, the study of covenant, and the daily unfolding of our marriage. The message: "Follow my words. Walk blameless before Me. Value and pursue righteousness as a visible sign of your obedience and love for Me. Let Me empty you of your impurities. Let Me give you a home."

A quotation I came across in our study of covenant pretty well describes what was taking place not only between God and each of us individually, but also between John and me.

A covenant of blood, a covenant made by the intercommingling of blood (or life forces), has been recognized as the closest, the holiest, and the most indissoluble, compact conceivable. Such a covenant clearly involves absolute surrender of one's separate self, and an irrevocable merging of one's individual nature into the dual, or the multiplied personality included in the compact. Man's highest and noblest outreachings of soul have, therefore, been for such a union with the divine nature as is typified in this human covenant of blood. (H. Clay Trumbull, *The Blood Covenant*, reprint edition [Kirkwood, Missouri: Impact Books, 1975.])

John and I were surrendering our separate selves to each other ănd to God. The ancient ceremony of covenant required the exchanging of robes, weapons, and belts. We were learning to do this. No, we weren't dressing in each other's clothes. We were exchanging *identities* by covering ourselves in love for each other (robes). I was no longer Patti Roberts or Patti—Me. Now, forever, I was bone of John's bone and flesh of his flesh, indissolubly part of him and he part of me. We were exchanging *friends and enemies* (weapons of warfare). Those who hated my husband hated me. Those who touched either of us in derision or enmity touched the other. We vowed to protect each other by using ourselves as a shield against whatever would come against the other. Whatever and whomever John loved came to live in my heart. Whatever and whomever I loved came to live in John's heart.

In a very real sense covenant partners also exchange Dun and Bradstreet reports and stock portfolios. All that I have (or have not), I give freely to my covenant partner, and he does likewise for me. That is true financially, emotionally, and physically.

The payoff in this new way of relating came as we realized again and again that John and I were not in this contract alone. There were three of us involved: God, John, and Patti. The three of us had formed a union. John and Patti were losing their identities and taking on God's. We were siding ourselves with those who loved Him and whom He loved. We could depend on God to defend our union as well as our lives and households. Just as we each took on the other's children forever, as if they were our own blood, so God took us all on as His forever-beloved family, a family for generations to come.

Just as we took on each other's assets and debt load, so God exchanged our paltry assets for the riches of His kingdom, spiritual as well as physical assets. We could trust Him to provide out of His storehouse of plenty for our needs.

And if I failed John in any way, John didn't have to fret and wonder, "What has she done to my life?" He could trust God to provide for him just what he needed.

If John failed me, ultimately I could *know* that, because the three of us were in contract with one another, God would take up the slack of John's failures. God would husband me.

So I no longer had to lay the burden of expectation solely on John. God and John shared responsibility for me. And in the areas in which we would inevitably fail each other, God would provide what we each needed.

It is easy, today, to think that basing one's spiritual life on an idea like covenant would be poor insurance indeed. And the idea of basing one's marriage on such a concept—well, that would be unthinkable. We live in a world in which everybody is looking for contracts that nail the other person down for sure. And we look for hidden back exits, built-in cushions, insurance in case of loss, to cover our backside. Covering one's own backside is a national obsession. Prenuptial agreements once entered into only by big stars and those with big money are now common legal documents for regular everyday folks. We all want to make sure we're taken care of just in case the marriage arrangement doesn't pan out.

God's way of marriage simply flies in the face of contemporary reason. By the example of Christ, He gives us a covenantal prenuptial (as well as mid- and postnuptial) agreement that might be worded like this:

> I freely offer to you and to God all of my spiritual and material wealth (past, present, and future, inclusive) for the express purpose of your becoming totally healthy and equipped in all dimensions of your being to live a full and satisfying life.

I agree that God may spend me in your behalf
in whatever way He deems proper.
In the spending of all my resources, we each
shall become the richer.

This is far too brief a look at the true implications of
God's covenant for our lives. John and I both
recommend a further investigation of the subject.
When we, as believers, finally realize that we are in a
pact with the Sovereign Lord of all, we begin to look at
life differently. We gain a different point of view.

Joining with each other and with God in a holy,
never-ending contract has assured us that, come what
may, we will be victorious, because, in spite of our
frailties and limitations, we are bonded to One who is all
strength and without limits. The only limit God could
possibly suffer in our lives would be the boundaries that
we, ourselves, put on His goodness due to our
unbelieving hearts. Therefore, we pray constantly,
"Lord, I believe . . . help Thou my unbelief."

As John and I were finishing our studies of
covenant with Debra Martin, and as we wrapped up the
writing of *El Shaddai*, the musical, I made a very
special request to God.

I had noticed that in all the biblical examples of
God's making a covenant with human beings—and
also with humans making covenants with one another—something was always given as part of the
sealing celebration.

Abraham and Sarah were given a son. I thought of
old Sarah, who had never conceived in her youth.
There she was at ninety, long since past her
menopausal years, her body settled into childlessness.
But not her spirit, because to seal the covenant, God
granted her a child.

Like Sarah, I had known infertility. In my
twenties, I was blessed by the adoption of little Christi;

she was truly a gift of love to me, and at age fifteen she still is. Her big brown eyes are windows into a soul so filled with the desire to love and be loved. In the years before she came to us, I took Clomid, a fertility drug. Upon her arrival, I stopped taking it, and two months later I became pregnant with Juli. I never knew if the Clomid suddenly kicked in or whether God just saw the lovely person Juli would become and knew that I couldn't live without her. These two girls have been a constant source of joy for me. Even in the lonely and troubled years of my life, they had such love to give and were so willing to receive the love I offered them. Both are lovely young women, growing up so fast, so bright, beautiful, and funny. Any woman would be proud to be their mother.

After Juli, I longed to have another child, but it was not to be. I went for many treatments, exams, and tests to help me conceive. But I could not.

When John and I married, suddenly I gained two more beautiful children. I have grown to cherish and enjoy Matt and Jessi, to love them as I do Christi and Juli. Our house and hearts have been filled with the laughter of children.

But my heart had a secret prayer: "God, if this union truly causes You pleasure, if it is really You that has blessed us with oneness, if You intend to show Your glory through our lives and our marriage, would You seal this covenant with a child? You know how old I am and how long I've been infertile. But will You cause me to bear a son? Father, please bless me with a son—a flesh-and-blood evidence of Your grace."

22

The Miracle of Forgiveness

Patti

*E*very family that wants to be a true family—blended and bonded together—has to have in operation some of the elements of covenant, even if they don't use biblical terms to describe their relationship. Trust, putting the other's welfare first, not requiring the other to fulfill all my needs, are some of those principles.

There is at least one other vital force that must be a part of a family if it is to last. *Forgiveness.* Forgiveness is the very foundation of enduring relationships. It is the only force that can rebuild the walls that the failure of love has torn down. Forgiveness begins as an act of our wills, but it is brought into completion through the infusion of God's nature into our hearts. Merely to will forgiveness is not enough. It is a beginning, true, but often the willingness doesn't last, because the will cannot change the condition of the wounded or the slighted heart.

We may will to pardon another, in a sense to grant a legal pardon, but the will can do nothing to erase the mental picture of the act that brought on the need to forgive. So we are left with the record of it in our mental and emotional archives. We may have forgiven, but we have not forgotten!

Yet, as we all know, to live successful, even healthy, lives, we must operate in forgiveness. As I have seen in my own life, as well as in the lives of others, we may talk a lot about forgiveness, but it remains an incomplete thing unless a miracle of heart occurs.

Our minister once told a kind of crazy story to illustrate the need for forgiveness. A man was asked by his wife each morning to take out the garbage. He was always willing to help, but rather than take it to the curb, where the refuse service could haul it off, he merely stashed each bag in the basement. After a while a putridly rotten smell came from the basement. That trash had been moved. It was out of sight, but it was still capable of contaminating the whole house.

Unless the process of forgiving is complete in us, we will be like the house with the basement full of garbage—contaminated.

When Mother Teresa visited Bhopal, India, after the tragic toxic leak from the Union Carbide plant there, her reaction to the terrible and extensive human damage and suffering was: "There is only one thing that can save Bhopal. . . . you must forgive"!

Greater than any other reconstructive force is the power that is released through complete forgiveness.

John and I needed so much to forgive, and to keep on forgiving. We had not only our own injuries to each other to consider, but also the injuries inflicted on our children. Yes, we *needed* to forgive. But *how* could we? Where were the real keys to put all of the truths we had learned into action? To know all about covenant and still have judgmentalism, bitterness, unforgiveness within us was like having the Concorde supersonic aircraft at the airport without any fuel. Nice idea, but no go!

First, we had to locate the blockages to forgiving. What was keeping the great warm rush of love from flowing out of our hearts to the other as it had when we were first married? And what was keeping us from forgiving others in our past who had hurt us?

One blockage is pride. We focus on *our* hurts and *our* feelings. We compare our deep hurt to the blackness of the other's sin. And self-pity is the running mate of pride. "What have I done that deserves such an injury?" we ask. "How could he or she possibly have been so mean to me?" Pride and pity are twins that keep us from realizing that our own hearts are clogged with self-righteousness.

I had a tendency to mentally replay John's bad-boy tapes every time I became hurt or disappointed. In these tapes he always looked damaged, beat-up, and sometimes just plain mean. I, on the other hand, looked ever the heroine of the melodrama, all done up in gauzy white tea dresses, the victim of his evil deeds. Though I knew these thoughts were lopsided and self-indulgent, I seemingly had no power to control them or to quit thinking them.

Debra Martin, our Bible teacher, was determined that I should begin to view both my thoughts and John's actions from a biblical perspective. At a heart level, she knew I was willing. But I needed some Scripture to hang on to. The word she gave me was Philippians 4:8.

> Finally, brethren, [and Sister Patti], whatever is true, whatever is honorable, whatever is just, whatever is pure, whatever is lovely, whatever is gracious, if there is anything worthy of praise, think about these things.

Debra would say to me, "Patti, when you begin to remember a painful or unjust happening, don't let that thought into the door of your mind. Frisk all thoughts at the door. Let in only the ones that can pass the Philippians 4:8 test. Remember, if it is pure enough to whisper into the ear of God, then it is healthy to think about."

Well, on certain days, that principle decreased my thought life down to nearly just my grocery list. It was an inner discipline that the Holy Spirit had to build within me.

During this time, Trish Hamilton, Jayne Ann Woods, and I continued our weekly prayer meetings. We each brought our prayer concerns, and when it came time to pray over mine, we would center on the spirit of self-righteousness that disrupted my ability to stay in forgiveness. If our financial problems had been taken care of immediately, as I had prayed they would be, I don't think the long and twisted "root of bitterness"—my self-righteousness and judgmentalism—would have been exposed. But God did expose it in all its crippling ugliness.

From my lofty perch, I had dispensed a lot of fleshly forgiveness to my dear John. But God required more, the real thing.

Finally I said to God, "Whatever it takes, free me of this ugly spirit."

Little by little God began to open my eyes to my real nature. I came to see myself not as a noble woman, obediently dispensing forgiveness, but as one who had deeply offended the merciful nature of God by remembering another's sin when my own heart held so many. And I began to view John's failures in a completely different light.

We are on the right track to forgiveness when our hearts are so moved and made tender by the hurt and brokenness that has caused someone to act against us in a destructive manner that we cry not for our own pain, but for that person's suffering and poverty of spirit. We cannot weep for our pain, but we must ask

God to so love the other person that we can intercede for his or her healing—heart, personality, spirit.

Forgiveness is the Christlike willingness to take on the other person's sin so that he or she doesn't have to bear the weight or the consequence of it. Real forgiveness, God's pure stream of forgiveness, will always cause us to love, without reservation, the offender so sincerely as to ache for his or her wholeness.

This kind of forgiveness infuses us with the radiant, life-giving personality of God. We become truly free. Self-righteousness and self-exaltation are not merely banned by this dying-through-the-power-of-love-for-another-person. They are finally destroyed.

This is the path of forgiveness I have set my feet on.

23

Signs of God's Love

Patti

*I*t was evident. God was restoring us as individuals and creating within the walls of our house a real home for all of us.

Nearly every day He sent us billboard-sized reminders of His union with us and of His wholesome intentions for us.

Even though the money problems were still a part of our lives, we had hopes of once and for all solving them. John's style of handling money was changing from "crisis management" to slow but steady reform. Our life-styles began to reflect a more thoughtful approach. The problems that we were still experiencing were more like the clean-up after a major earthquake than a series of aftershocks that crippled our ability to maintain equilibrium. Clean-up was a process, but it reflected steady progress. As far as finances went, it seemed that when we absolutely had to have a certain amount by a certain hour of a certain day, it would be there. It might often be 11:59:59 on the clock of desperation, but El Shaddai, our covenant God, let us know that we could depend on Him.

We found that He had such ingenious ways of

saying, "Hang on. I love you. It's all going to work out."

God's love messages are often as plentiful as His blessings. And among our blessings are friends. Two of our special friends are Peter and Barbara Jenkins. About a year and a half after we were married, the four of us drove down to Atlanta together and spent the four-hour drive talking about the book John and I wanted to write—about becoming a family and overcoming the negative inheritances from the past as we were being blended together. Peter and Barbara are both successful authors and had good advice for us. Barbara felt that there was a place for a book about the blending of families, and in her mind we were qualified to address the subject.

While Barbara and I chatted in the back seat about all of this, John and Peter, in the front seat, had decided that Peter would be our literary agent. By the time we returned from Atlanta, Peter had big plans for us and for the book.

Not long after that, we scheduled a brunch at our house to talk about the book with a publisher. I hadn't been feeling too well for several weeks, but we decided to go ahead with the brunch. By 7:30 that morning, the day was already hectic. The girl who was going to help me clean the house phoned to say she couldn't come until that afternoon. I'd just have to do the cleaning and the brunch preparation myself.

Still, because I hadn't felt well for some time, John and I decided I should take one of those early pregnancy tests. We had laughed as we bought it because, of all the things that might be wrong with me, it seemed that, given my inability to conceive, pregnancy was the least likely. So, on the morning of the publisher's meeting, I took the test. The procedure is brief, and the results are visible in a couple of hours. While I waited, I went to the grocery store to buy brunch supplies. Pregnancy was a farfetched idea; besides, I felt awfully crampy.

John helped me unload the four or five bags of groceries from the car, and I flew into high gear. I was dipping big red strawberries into melted white chocolate when I remembered the test and went to check it. There on the bathroom windowsill was a positive test.

The doorbell rang as I went to find John. He was letting Peter in, who'd arrived early to go over some of the details of the meeting. I asked John to come into our bedroom. "Honey, what's wrong?" he asked as he closed the door.

"The EPT indicates that I'm pregnant," I told him. "But there must be some other explanation. Let's call the doctor."

John called our doctor's office, only to be told that home tests are quite accurate and if it indicated a pregnancy then there most likely was a pregnancy!

"A baby . . . a baby! We're going to have a baby!" John sat on the edge of the bed, repeating those words as he stared into space. He looked neither happy nor sad—just stunned.

I had never told John of my prayer for God to send us a son as a sign of His sealing our covenant with Him, even though I had thought that the strange physical sensations I'd felt these last few weeks might indeed be His answer to that prayer.

When we told Peter our news, he let out a yell and started to dance around the living room, his cowboy boots making a loud rhythm track to dance by. He was positively ecstatic.

The brunch was quickly reduced from a large scrumptious menu to self-serve chocolate-covered strawberries and coffee. I couldn't do anything but rest my precious cargo on the sofa and grin at my stunned husband.

After the meeting, we rushed to the doctor's office for a blood test—we had to know for *sure!* "What's the hurry?" the nurse asked. All I could do was shake my head, and smile, and reply, "When you are thirty-eight and have teenaged children at home and are infertile and have a husband on the verge of passing out, it is just important to know these things quickly."

When the phone call came, the voice on the other end of the line said, "Well, Mrs. Thompson, you're going to have a baby. Congratulations!"

I hung up the phone and patted my stomach, saying to myself, *This isn't just a baby. This is my son—my covenant child.*

Then I ran down the hall yelling at the top of my voice, "John, Juli, Christi, we've got to call Matt and Jessi. It's confirmed. He's coming!"

24

The
Dance of the Broken Heart

Patti

*F*or the next several months we busied ourselves with the wonderful task of waiting. Waiting for movement. Waiting for kicks. Waiting for labor pains. Waiting for birth.

As my womb grew and grew—and grew!—so did my sense of being fat with contentment and wonder. Often I would pat my stomach, bless the baby, and tell him how dearly I loved him. Each evening as John and the children would hug and kiss me goodnight, they, too, would pat my stomach and say, "Goodnight, precious baby."

We waited. And we wrote.

When we began this book, we laid out dozens of titles to consider and finally settled on *Dance of the Broken Heart*. We loved the title because it suggests that God can cause even that which has known brokenness to dance again. It speaks of celebration after trauma. But as the writing and the living of the writing progressed, a deeper meaning began to come to life.

We began to know that the heart we were both to talk about and to experience had not been broken solely by injury or pain. It is a heart that has experienced an explosion of love so powerful that it has burst open, and so has enlarged its capacity.

The most beautiful dance that we wounded mortals can dance is the one that flows from brokenness. It is a dance of praise that flows from a broken heart emptied of self, ambition, independence. A heart from which the thorns of anger, self-preoccupation, and self-devotion have been pulled. A heart from which the roots of rage against all that threatens self-governing have been removed.

The broken heart forever leaks, drips, and pours forth what is poured into it. It never again can contain solely for itself anything that is poured into it. Where once it was a reservoir, now it is a river—a passageway for love, health, and beauty to flow from the throne room, to the bedroom, kitchen, children's rooms, living room, and then on to pulpit, offices, classrooms, and to the world.

This heart has a love that is committed to healing action. It is not dependent upon the momentary flowering of romance. The flower of romance buds, blooms, fades, dies, and rests, then perhaps buds and blooms again. It comes and goes depending on the season. But the healing love of the broken heart endures in all seasons.

None of this comes easily. The living out of this love is so demanding, so life-threatening, that it doesn't really occur without daily trips to the cross.

Several years ago I prayed, "Oh, God, teach me how to love." I was aware that although I had once been married, and although I had known romance, I still knew very little about loving. When John and I met and fell in love, God began answering that prayer. But not at all in the way I expected.

There is a consensus of thought that love comes to us, warms us, ignites us, inspires us, and pours goodness and healing into us. We tend to think of love as a warm bubble bath—washing and soothing away all our wounds, enlarging us, heaping the wonders of life upon us, giving and giving and giving to us.

Perhaps, ultimately, love does these things. But first it requires the entire emptying of self in order to create a home for this incoming love. And the emptying of self is such a costly and painful thing, most people simply don't have the wherewithal, the stamina, to go through it. When the process is complete, the heart no longer exists to *receive* love. It exists, rather, to *become* love for those God puts in its path. In becoming love it finds fulfillment.

Apart from the courage that Christ imparts, that kind of love is not possible.

For John and me, the call to this kind of love consumed any brittle religiosity we might have been carrying and called us to genuineness. The self-givingness of the Lord of the cross by His passionate presence wooed us not only to express our own love for each other, but also to ache for the other's healing, wholeness, and freedom. We began to yearn for the other's total health. Each time we fell from this goal and reacted to former injuries or referred back to failures, a definite smell of rotting flesh permeated our relationship.

The story of Christ's raising Lazarus from the dead has a point that can be applied here. When Jesus stood at his friend's tomb and ordered his dead friend to come forth, Lazarus came out of that tomb—alive. But after four days of death, he was still wrapped in the burial garments that, by this time, had become the stinking evidence of death. Jesus had to tell the stunned crowd around the tomb to remove the grave clothes from Lazarus and let him go free.

We are to do this in our families. After we have been forgiven and given back our lives—restored to love—we must remove the grave clothes of the remembrance of their failures. The act of removing them transforms the one who helps unwind the clothes just as surely as it does the one who is bound.

For us and for other families being blended by God, the process has an added dimension. Just as we must strip the death linen from each other, we must also strip it from our memories of our former spouses.

John

When we were writing the songs for our first album together, Patti and I worked on an idea that developed into the song "Outposts": *Godly homes are just outposts of the kingdom.* This concept of home and family has been a consistent thread running through everything we have experienced and created during our first three years of marriage.

Imagine a small, weary band of soldiers, dirty, injured, afraid. Picture them after a long march through enemy territory, stopping to rest on a hillside. It is dark. In the distance they see the light from a friendly campfire . . . an outpost.

The word *outpost* is defined as a detachment of troops stationed at a distance from the main unit. That is what *home* is for the Christian. Our families are the places where we experience the kingdom of God within four walls. Our eternal home—the main unit—is with God in heaven. Our earthly homes are outposts of the kingdom.

The family is the place where God desires to make His stand against darkness. From Genesis to Revelation, we see how important family is to God. He chose to establish the family as the unit of existence around which all creation revolves. Even the animal kingdom mirrors this. The importance of the family is shown in the fact that to destroy it, sin began within the family unit, thus setting in motion forever the course of divine restoration.

God will make His home forever with a restored family. His covenant with Abraham resulted in the promise of a family—the family of blessing from which all the families of the earth will be blessed. His deliverance of the family of Israel from bondage in Egypt resulted in the establishment of a homeland. In the ultimate confirmation of the family, God sent the inestimable gift of His only Son into the world as part of a human family. That gift resulted in the breaking, once and for all, of the power of sin, opening the door of eternal life, so that we can become part of the eternal family. Each human family has the possibility of reflecting the promise of His eternal family.

God desires wholeness. He desires restoration. He does not desire divorce, for that killing form of survival is an invention of the Enemy. Though millions of us have experienced divorce, for millions of varied reasons, it does not mitigate the fact that it is not God's way of solving marital problems. So where does God stand in the face of all these human mess-ups?

To redeem our damaged lives, he chooses to stand on the side of forgiveness and restoration—a restoration that includes all damaged parties.

Patti and I have four precious children between us from our previous marriages. Thus the children have necessary allegiances to parents other than us. Juli and Christi have Richard and Lindsay Roberts, and also a beautiful little black-haired half sister, Jordon. Matthew and Jessica have Mike and Kathleen Jones as part of their lives. We are eleven people whose lives are, in very real terms, intertwined.

In all honesty, however, I must say that I am not considering holding a family reunion with all of these I have named. But as Christians, we all must move to forgiveness and wholeness as God leads us. The wars of the parents must not be fought with the children as ammunition. In practical terms, I have no particular urge to spend time with the Roberts or the Jones families, and they probably would feel awkward with the Thompsons. But in equally practical terms, I must lift up Richard to Christi and Juli and pray for God's restoration to continue in Richard's family as well as in ours. The same goes for Matt and Jessi's mother, Kathleen. With all rhetoric and songs and sermons aside, all of us who are in Christ look forward to spending eternity together. That means the Robertses, the Thompsons, and the Joneses and all our various children are to be one in God, as are all the other fragmented families and people whom God has taken to himself. But it simply cannot happen without Christ's working His forgiveness and healing in us and through us.

Patti

We do not look for healing or love in our families or try to forgive past wrongs merely to insure ourselves a place in heaven. Nor can our motive be to make our families run successfully or to escape the moral and physical consequences of harboring negative emotions. Our motive must be nothing less than to know and experience God at a deeper level.

Our marriage, as it heals, ripens, and reaches its earthly potential, is to be a miniature foretaste of an event yet to come. To that end, God has exposed us to the wonderful truths of His covenant with us, the study of which has unveiled His nature to us and has allowed us to trust Him to be God. The healing of generational sins in our lives, as well as the deliverance from demonic strongholds, has set the stage for the same blessed event.

The hardships we have experienced, financial as well as relational, had hidden benefits. They helped us shed our spirits of independence. We had been living, thinking, deciding, and acting apart from God's counsel. He was removing from us that part of our lives in which we chose to separate ourselves from Him. At times it has seemed so harsh that we have cried, "God, why us? Were our sins so horrible as to generate this type of reaping? Now you are even asking us to lay down our own methods of survival."

God's mercy was that He responded to our prayer for restoration, a prayer that, unbeknownst to us, included this invitation to slay our independent selves. He did this through a stripping so radical it could be termed violent. We have balked at being so stripped, so without alternatives or other courses of action. We have had no option but to wholly lean on Him, not only for our righteousness, but for everything else as well. We have had to come to Him like babies crying for our milk, our comfort, our shelter. *El Shaddai* is no longer merely an Amy Grant hit, but is what the name means—our Refuge, our Sustenance, our Promise-keeper. God's intentions were not to deprive us or to bring us to judgmental poverty, but to expose the poverty and deprivation that exists when we are not in every portion of our beings intertwined in His thoughts and provision.

All that we have experienced since June 1983, God has allowed in order to disentangle us from the tentacles of our willful idolatry of a world system that elevates human will above God. I suspect that the intent of God's dealings with us would have been the same, whether we had lived circumspect lives or had fallen even lower than we did fall. God wants to remove all that keeps us from trusting Him—including our sin, our self-sufficiency, our unforgiveness, our guilt, and even our religiousness.

With clear sight, we can now read the invitation God has sent to us. It is engraved in blood, in tears, and in joy. It invites John and Patti Thompson to move freely and gracefully and with reckless abandon to throw ourselves into the eternal task of loving Christ and experiencing Him in each other. It is also an invitation to build a home within the walls of heaven and heaven within the walls of our home.

Finally, it is an invitation to dance the dance of love. A dance that joyfully anticipates that soon-coming event: union finally with Christ.

It is a prophetic dance. A bridal dance.

The dance of the broken heart.

25

Canon

John

---

*T*hey dressed me in a white suit that made me look as if I were going to clean a nuclear reactor, complete with hat and shoe covers! Patti and I had been to the hospital three times, but we knew this was *the* one. The first time was almost three weeks before, when Patti had gone into premature labor. They told us that we were about a half hour from delivery, and she was given medication to stop the labor, because the baby was seven weeks early.

Patti had to stay in the hospital for a week that time, so that they both could be monitored. During that week, we saw the baby on an electronic monitor and learned that, without a doubt, it was a boy.

At the end of the week we were sent home. The doctor told Patti that she should be in bed until Canon arrived, which, since it was the middle of December, left me with exactly 100 percent of the Christmas shopping to do, along with recording the musical. To our aid came the ladies of our church, who provided many meals, and my mother, Caroline, who arrived to help keep it all together.

I had known that the due date was January 22, but

secretly I hoped the doctor was off enough to let Jessica and Matthew see the baby. They arrived on December 26. The flight from Anchorage is like an overseas flight, almost eight hours in the air, but we had our Christmas celebration late that night. Everyone was too excited at being together to sleep. We have learned to treasure these times with all of the family assembled and count them as a blessing from God. Matthew and his cousin, Christopher, stayed up all night, leaving them out of commission for most of the next day. The gifts and cookies from Grandma's kitchen were wonderful, but everyone seemed preoccupied with the impending arrival of Canon. The only disagreements were over who would get to hold him and when. Even now God was using this little one to blend us and bind us all closer together.

On Saturday evening, December 28, Patti had been having regular pains for a few hours, and her doctor said to come to the hospital. This time we had a regular exodus to the hospital: Patti and I, Juli, Jessica, Matthew, Christi, Harold and Caroline (my parents), Carol and Christopher (my sister and nephew). It was a long night, and the nurse finally told us it was probably false labor. We could stay or go home, she said. It was up to us.

We went home. The entourage followed. On the way home, Patti graphically described what condition she would have to be in for us to go back!

The next night at 11:40 Patti had a pain that woke us both from a sound sleep. Her requirements had been met! She and I went on to the hospital, leaving my parents and sister to bring the children. At 2:45 I donned my white suit and picked up a very large tape recorder that Patti insisted on, and we entered the delivery room. The delivery—and the recording—were without complication. What a blessing had been given to us! Canon Gray Thompson, 2:57 A.M., December 30, 1985.

Canon. The name means a rod with which to measure straightness. We named him Canon to celebrate the righteous acts God was doing in our lives.

Canon was given to me by the nurse to carry to the nursery. I left the delivery room and started down a forty-yard hallway. In the small windows set in the swinging doors at the end of the hall, I could see Christi's face on one side and Jessica's appearing about every other second in the other as she jumped up to see. When Christi saw that I was carrying the baby, I could read her lips as she shouted to the rest of the family, "He has the baby!" I had the joy of walking through the excited family, all trying to get their first look. Within a few minutes, they were all glued to the windows of the nursery, watching Canon have his first bath.

I am not the type to pull out pictures of my children from my wallet without being asked. However, I feel the need to thank God through the medium of this book, for the miracle of birth, in this time, to these people. It is surely an act of restoration, covenant, and grace.

Just after 6:00 A.M., when the others had gone home to sleep, Patti and I were given a few minutes together with Canon. He was only 4 pounds, 11 ounces, but filled with promise. And in perfect condition, the doctors had said.

When I left the hospital later that morning the sky was a brilliant orange and gray, with the sun still below the horizon. One of the tall buildings on the Nashville skyline had the words *Happy New Year* spelled in five-story letters in its windows. It would be.

Tonight I had seen in the eyes of the children— Matthew, Juli, Jessica, Christi, and their cousin, Christopher—some of the truth that God had intended: that this new little boy had come to join those five little battle-scarred hearts (and the older ones too), not to replace or dim the other families they were a part of, but to add a measure of God's grace to their lives, to continue the process of bonding, blessing, and blending.

And the glory of the Lord is again revealed in a baby.

Epilogue

Navarre Beach, Florida
Spring 1986

Patti

I'm staring out the sliding glass doors at the blackened horizon. Intense streaks of lightning have slit the sky like laser knives. Thunder muffles the sounds of the waves as they crash and befuddle the white sand. Let the storm tear and threaten and bully the earth. I'm inside, all safe and warm and wonderfully complete.

What a startling contrast all of this is to my last visit to this beach. It amazes me how the same condominium, the same bedroom, the same bed, the same everything can be so very different.

Juli, Christi, and I came here four years ago to work on my last book, *Ashes to Gold*. The writing was going fairly well, and the children were playing happily, when a storm suddenly blew in and they came inside. In order to find a quiet place to work, I went downstairs to my bedroom, the same room in which I am now writing. Since writing at a desk is foreign to me, I piled up the pillows and plopped myself and my legal pad into bed.

The sounds of the storm uncovered an unutterably lonely place in me, the kind of loneliness that makes one weak with grief. My writing materials slid onto the floor as I drew myself up into the fetal position. I loved my children devotedly, and they gave me surely as much comfort as I gave them mothering. But as wonderful as our relationships were, they couldn't compete with this stalking ache of loneliness. *Will my heart ever know union with another?* I wondered. *Or will my singleness stretch out endlessly before me like the ocean outside the window?* The thought of that caused me to turn my head into my pillow and scream.

How different this storm is! It is just a storm, not a display of sorrow.

The bed in which I sit, propped up with four pillows, is the transient and happy nest of two people in love.

Upstairs Christi and Juli are preparing a dinner of ham omelets and fried potatoes. John, my husband and best friend, looks rather professorial with his tortoise shell glasses perched on the end of his nose, sitting cross-legged on the floor, pounding away at his computer terminal, writing his segments of this book.

Canon, our four-month-old son, having nursed himself into a sound sleep, is sacked out on the sofa.

We have already made plans for the whole family to return to this very condo and have a bang-up holiday when Matt and Jessi arrive home from Alaska this summer.

The bills have all been paid, and our musical has already been successfully performed—twice. Once at St. Bartholomew's Episcopal Church on Good Friday, and again on April 1 at Musi, California (a yearly convention for church choral directors).

"And what of tickets, Mrs. Thompson?" you might ask. "What about your beloved tickets?"

Well, I have been laid off from the circuit of service outside my home. I don't really know if that is temporary or forever. But I do know that anything apart from my day-to-day obedience to the call of love is superfluous. There is so little I can figure out any more. But I am figuring out the life of love.

If I have any objection to revealing our circumstances to you, the reader, it is that I realize that all we are discovering is still fresh and new and still untempered by decades of being married to each other. Our marriage, even with all these failures, resolutions, and hope, is only three-and-one-half years old. There will be other "roots" of sin that we will discover as the Holy Spirit continually draws us into the light of truth. There will be more pain, and there will be more healing. These are facts that those who open themselves to the refiner's fire must reckon with.

But we are being given tools to grow in His grace with each other.

Some might say, "How do you know that this marriage won't end in failure?"

All I can answer is that we trust in His continually manifested grace toward us, and as we are individually bonded to God, we shall surely remain bonded to each other.

In the great thundering noise outside, I hear God speak. He tells me that He heals broken hearts. That He causes them to dance. That He makes all things new.

Indeed He does.

You may write to John and Patti at the following address:

John and Patti Thompson
P. O. Box 1129
Franklin, Tennessee 37064

All letters will be read . . . and some will even be answered (as time and staff are available).